The Research Journal

A Reflective Tool for Your First
Independent Research Project

Barbara Bassot

First published in Great Britain in 2020 by
Policy Press
University of Bristol
1-9 Old Park Hill
Bristol
BS2 8BB
UK
t: +44 (0)117 954 5940
pp-info@bristol.ac.uk
www.policypress.co.uk

North America office:
Policy Press
c/o The University of Chicago Press
427 East 60th Street
Chicago, IL 60637, USA
t: +1 773-702-7700
f: +1 773-702-9756
sales@press.uchicago.edu
www.press.uchicago.edu

British Library Cataloguing in Publication Data
A catalogue record for this book is available from the British Library
Library of Congress Cataloging-in-Publication Data
A catalog record for this book has been requested

ISBN 978-1-4473-5278-5 paperback
ISBN 978-1-4473-5280-8 ePdf

Interior design by Liron Gilenberg | www.ironicitalics.com
Cover design by blu inc
Front cover credit: Stocksy/Wizemark
Printed and bound in Great Britain by TJ International, Padstow
Policy Press uses environmentally responsible print partners

Contents

Acknowledgements

I would like to express my sincere thanks to my family and friends for all their support in the process of bringing *The Research Journal* to fruition. In particular I would like to thank Martin Bassot for his careful work on the diagrams and Marc Bassot for his proofreading and constructive comments. I would also like to thank the reviewers of the proposal and typescript whose positive and helpful comments helped me to develop the work into the book it has become. I would especially like to thank my Commissioning Editor, Catherine Gray, for her belief in the project and for her support, and to the publisher for being prepared to take a risk with a new kind of publication.

Introduction

Welcome to *The Research Journal*. You are probably reading this because you are about to start or have recently started your first piece of independent research. You might well be studying at undergraduate level. However, if you are doing a Master's programme and you didn't undertake a research element at undergraduate level, you may well find this book useful too. Whatever your current situation, *The Research Journal* is designed as a practical tool to help you to succeed in each aspect of your research project through the process of critical reflection. Any first piece of independent research is a very big and challenging undertaking; this journal will help you to see the whole picture (often very difficult to visualise in the early stages) and the individual parts that make up the whole. This means you will be able to manage your research project well; no one else will be able to do this for you, and it will ensure your success. The journal will also help you to reflect on your learning and progress throughout your research project and will enable you to write a dissertation you can be proud of.

Who this journal is for

The Research Journal is designed for all students who are doing their first piece of independent research. This is often a key piece of assessed work that needs to be submitted towards the end of a programme of study. Because of its size and the number of credits it carries, it can have a significant impact on your overall grade or degree classification. Because of this, many students recognise its importance and want to do well in it. Independent research often gives you the opportunity to focus on a subject or topic you are interested in and enables you to delve deeper and learn more about it. A discussion of your dissertation is common at interviews for jobs and graduate schemes because of the variety of skills you develop during the process. Critical reflection lies at the heart of a high-quality dissertation and this book's journal format enables you to engage with the necessary metaprocesses (thinking about thinking) to critically evaluate your growing knowledge and understanding. As a result, it puts you firmly in charge of your research.

How to use this book

The Research Journal is practical in nature and is designed as a reflective tool to help you engage critically with each aspect of your research project and to take control of it. In the early stages, you will probably feel very enthusiastic about your study and it is good to capitalise on this. As time progresses, you might begin to feel pressurised by the scale of the task, especially as it often comes at a time when you have lots of other academic work to complete, and maybe final examinations to prepare for too. This journal can help you to manage the process effectively and will help in the inevitable ups and downs of the research process.

You will probably have been given a significant length of time for working on your research project; this can be comforting, yet deceptive at the same time. In the early days it is all too easy to think that you have plenty of time, and procrastination can quickly set in as you sit back and start to put things off. Before you know it, weeks have gone by and the deadline starts to feel much closer. Then feelings of panic can start to surface, which can make people feel overwhelmed and even stuck, so making progress can sometimes start to get tricky. This book has a strong emphasis on planning, which helps to prevent a range of negative feelings associated with completing a large assessed project. You have probably already been asked to write essays, as well as other types of written work. This book will help you

to keep up the writing habit and includes activities that help you to reflect on what you are achieving in this area. It also helps you to understand more about yourself and how you can manage your project well.

This is not a book on research methods or on completing a research project, as there are plenty of those available. What it does provide is a practical and reflective tool to use as a 'how to', alongside other texts which focus on the academic and practical aspects of social research. During your independent study you are likely to find a small number of what you will come to know as your go-to books on research methods; you might even find one to use as your first point of reference. This is good and likely to be very helpful to you in the research process. *The Research Journal* is a book to use together with these, not instead of them, because it is designed to help you to establish your direction and work through the process. In the early stages of a project, many students say they struggle to find their feet and using this book at this time can be particularly effective. You will also want to use it to keep a record of your work and thoughts on the whole research process, and this could prove particularly valuable if you are asked to write a reflective evaluation of your work either as part of your dissertation or as a separate piece. Ultimately how you use this book is up to you because it is all about you and your learning; this is an individual thing. However, here are some pointers to bear in mind:

- It is very practical, and you will gain the most from it by engaging with the activities rather than simply reading them. The process of completing the activities encourages you to think at a deeper level at every step. This means that as time progresses you should find your understanding of the research process grows and your knowledge of your chosen topic develops.

- It is designed as a book you write in, so please do so. Remember, you can always supplement the space for writing with a blank notebook or a document on your favourite device.

- Overall the content is structured to follow the research process. However, there isn't one single way of completing a research project. This means it may well be helpful to skim the book first and then dip in and out of it as you see fit. You will probably gain more from using it like this rather than mechanically working through it from start to finish. Indeed, there is something contradictory about engaging with free-flow writing in a very structured way, as you will see in Theme 1.1.

- There are some reminders of aspects of study skills; if you know you are strong in these areas, feel free to skip them. But, if you've had feedback comments such as, 'You need to continue working on your academic language' and 'Your referencing is still not especially accurate', these could be useful in helping you to get the mark you hope for.

Overall, this is a book that you will want to keep close at hand as your project progresses. The benefits of using it vary from person to person, but include:

- It contains accessible, bite-sized content on areas that can be difficult to understand initially.
- It guides you through the research process.
- It contains space for your own reflections.

3

- It helps you to develop your knowledge in the area of research generally and in relation to your chosen topic area.
- It helps you to take control of your research project.

Of course, none of these aspects of the book can guarantee you a higher mark, but they can help you to succeed.

The role of writing in research and learning

Many tutors and supervisors encourage their students to keep a reflective journal as part of the research process, but few give advice on how to do this effectively to get the most from it. In higher education, there is growing evidence of the value of journal writing in aiding students' development, and here are some of the reasons why. Journal writing helps us to:

- Gain new insights and develop our understanding. It is difficult to write about something well unless we understand what we are writing about. If we don't understand what we have written, probably no one else will either!

- Slow down and think at a significantly deeper level. Most of us live life at a fast pace, and slowing down is important for developing our critical thinking. We need to give ourselves time and space to do this.

- Examine where we stand on things as a researcher. If we have not made our own position in the research clear, it may open us up to criticisms of subjectivity and bias and it will fail to stand up to the academic rigour of assessment.

- Engage with the research process in a more transparent way. Any dissertation or research project needs to be open and transparent in relation to how it has been carried out, so that its validity can be assessed.

- Make an accurate record of each aspect of our research. It is all too easy to think that we will remember relevant detail, when, in practice, this doesn't always happen. This becomes problematic as our research progresses, and we need to look back and write about what we did and why. In addition, we probably all remember times when we have been writing a piece of work and need to refer to something that we have read, but don't remember where we read it. We then have to spend lots of time trying to find it again, often at a time when the deadline is looming! (Borg, 2001; Ortlipp, 2008; Bassot, 2016).

The first of these bullet points is particularly worth noting; we write about things in order to understand them, rather than because we already understand them. This helps us to see why starting to write is often the most difficult part; it means we need to write when there is probably a lot that we don't yet understand. However, it is the act of writing itself that helps our understanding and knowledge to grow, so it is important not to put it off. The best piece of advice I ever received when doing my doctoral studies was, 'Don't get it right, get it written!' At first this advice felt like turning everything on its head as I felt I needed to understand things before I could write about them. But being prepared to take the advice proved to be an important step forward because, once I started to write, things began to get easier and I understood more. Unlike many of the books you have used at university so far, *The Research Journal* is one that you are asked to write

in – so please do so, as it provides some ideal steps towards understanding more.

Research terminology
Terminology in research is by its very nature abstract and, as a result, it can be difficult to grasp and potentially confusing. Theme 5 explores some key terms. When writing this book, some key decisions were made in relation to its scope and the terminology used; these are summarised here.

There are regular debates among academic staff in the social sciences about appropriate content for research methods modules. These modules are commonly studied at undergraduate and postgraduate level. Some academics (but not all) agree that undergraduate students need some grasp of methodology at a philosophical level, often demonstrated through a discussion of different research paradigms. Others argue that at this level an understanding of the difference between quantitative and qualitative research is sufficient. This is the approach taken by writers such as Greetham (2019) and Cottrell (2014) as shown by the content of their publications. These academics take the stance that postgraduate students then need more, including a grasp of areas like constructivism, critical theory, ethnography, grounded theory, narrative, phenomenology and case study, as the content of Biggam's (2018) text demonstrates. The approach taken in this book is that, for undergraduate study, having a grasp of the philosophical positions of positivism and interpretivism and the differences between quantitative and qualitative research will equip students well for their studies. So, this means that if your particular research methods module includes other philosophical aspects as highlighted earlier, or if you are studying at postgraduate level, you will need to add your own reflections on these aspects to your journal entries.

In addition, some research terminology is potentially confusing, especially the terms 'method' and 'methods'. These particular terms are often used interchangeably in published literature. For the purpose of clarity in this book, and in response to feedback from other educators in higher education, they are used in this way: the term 'method' in the singular is used to refer to the choice of approach to research, whether quantitative or qualitative. The term 'methods' in the plural is used to refer to more specific

techniques that researchers use to carry out their studies, such as questionnaires, interviews and observations.

A decision was also made not to use two particular terms in relation to research. First, the term 'research objectives', which usually refers to the specific things that someone is trying to achieve (or even answers they are trying to find) by carrying out their study. In this book the term 'research questions' is used because in the social sciences research often involves gaining insights and understandings rather than specific outputs. Second, the term 'research strategy' has also not been used. This is an umbrella term that encompasses each aspect of the design of your study; the focus in this book is on each aspect of your research. However, you will need to be strategic at all times in your approach in order to succeed.

Outline of contents

The Research Journal is organised in two parts. Part 1 has ten themes, each focusing on a particular issue or area. These themes have short pieces of relevant content, broken down into subsections, with reflective activities to complete to enable you to develop your critical thinking, your ideas and your work. They are designed to take you through the research process from start to completion, with Theme 1 focusing on the beginning of the research process through to Theme 10 on submission and review. However, please remember that, in doing a research project, there is no single correct order in which to do things and sometimes the process can feel quite cyclical. Each theme starts with a brief introduction and is followed by five pieces of content based on the theme, where some key issues, theories and helpful approaches are introduced. There are also a number of practical activities and some space for writing your reflections. Towards the end of each theme there is a larger activity to carry out to help you to cement your understanding further.

Based on feedback received and on my own work, students often need help to understand what a research journal might look like. Part 1 contains extracts from Alex's journal, a student who is carrying out a project on single-use plastic and its effects on the environment. These journal extracts serve two purposes: to show how the student's understanding develops through the use of journal writing and to give an example of what a research journal might look like. However, any research journal is very much an individual thing, so remember that you will need to develop your

own style of reflective writing. This means resisting the temptation to follow this example too closely, assuming that because it is in this book this is how you should do it. Each theme concludes with a top tip to help you succeed in your studies or a case study example.

Part 2 focuses on your own particular research project; it is more personal to you and is structured in seven sections around a series of key questions for you to reflect on in relation to your own work. Many students struggle with moving from the generalities of a research methods module to applying what they have learned to their own project, and this section is designed to help you to do this. The questions in Part 2 will help you as you work through the research process and will provide an important record that you can return to when you get to the writing-up stage. There are more top tips and case studies here too. At the end of the journal you will find a list of references.

I hope that you find *The Research Journal* helpful at this vital stage of your academic development. Good luck and here's to your successful graduation!

Part 1

Engaging in the research process

Part 1 is divided into ten themes and is designed to take you on a reflective journey through the process of doing your first piece of research from start to completion. But don't forget that the journey is yours and how you navigate it (for example, from Theme 1 to Theme 10 in sequence, or in a different order according to your learning and development needs) is entirely up to you. Taking some time to complete the reflective activities will ensure that you think through each step along the way.

Theme 1

Journal writing

This section will:

- help you to understand what a research journal looks like;

- enable you to understand more about the importance of journal writing;

- help you to make the link between writing and understanding;

- help you to start writing reflectively in relation to your research;

- introduce you to a model for reflective writing.

What does a research journal look like?

On the surface this sounds like a simple enough question but delve a little deeper and it's not necessarily as easy as it appears. A quick internet search shows that people do not necessarily agree on what a research journal should look like, and indeed there are views that appear to be at opposite extremes: there are those who see it as a place to take brief notes, primarily in relation to sources (for example, books, journal articles) and others who advocate keeping a record of everything! Most support the idea of writing in it regularly but are much less clear on what to write. The words 'journal', 'diary' and 'log' are sometimes used interchangeably, which can also be confusing. In general, these three terms tend to mean different things:

- **Journal** – this often means a place for free-flow writing. Some people keep a personal journal where they write about their everyday lives; others keep a journal for a specific purpose, for example for a project or during their travels. In everyday life, a journal can often take the form of a nice quality notebook where you can write freely about whatever you have decided to focus on. A journal can also be used as a place to keep other things, such as photographs, diagrams and lists. Initially most of the pages will probably be blank.

- **Diary** – this tends to be calendar-driven with specific dates listed, and there are a variety of options to choose from (for example, a week to view on each page or a week spread across two pages); it will often include planners for the month or year. There will also be space to write, but this can restrict your writing to the amount of space given.

- **Log** – this is a basic record of events, often kept in date order. It is generally factual – a list of what you did and when.

So, what will be the most useful as you start your first piece of independent research? It is likely that there will be aspects of each of these kinds of records that you will want to capitalise on in order to make it work for you. Free-flow writing in a journal will help your ideas and understanding to develop (see Theme 1.3). This could be prompted by things like reading texts that you feel are key to your research, discussions with your supervisor, things you discover as you gather your data,

Notes

among others. Diary aspects will be particularly helpful for planning (see Theme 3.1), which will help you to keep on track and not lose sight of what you need to do and when. A log will ensure that you can find things quickly and easily (see Table 3 on page 57), such as those all-important references. This book is designed to help you to do all of these things, so feel free to use it in the way it helps you most.

The importance of journal writing

Many people in universities are beginning to see the value of journal writing and recognise that it can help students in various areas of their academic and personal development. Here are some of the reasons for this, and you may be able to think of more:

- **It helps us to slow down** – we all need time to develop our critical thinking, and writing in a journal provides us with the scope to do this more effectively.

- **It helps to externalise things** – if we spend too long thinking, things can start to go round and round in our heads, which can make us feel confused and overwhelmed. Writing in a journal gets our thoughts out on to paper, and often makes our heads feel clearer as a result.

- **It's a place for offloading** – all research has its ups and downs, and a journal can be a place for articulating our feelings, particularly when things don't go according to plan. This helps us to cope with stress and deal with anxiety.

- **It helps us to keep on track** – most of us know that in order to succeed we need a plan; hence the well-known phrase, 'To fail to plan is to plan to fail'. A journal can be a secure place (more secure than a piece of paper that we can lose) for our research plans.

- **It provides us with a record that we can go back to** – most of us think that we will remember things, particularly when it is something significant. Unfortunately, everyday life is hectic, and we can't remember everything; sometimes even important things can escape our memory.

- **It helps us to question our assumptions** – taking a questioning approach to journal writing (see Theme 1.5) can help us to address issues of subjectivity and bias in our research.

- **It makes us accountable to ourselves** – a good supervisor will want to know about the progress we are making, but the progress we make will always be down to us. Keeping a journal means that we can keep a check on ourselves; for example, how far we have achieved our goals and what we need to do next.

Notes

Journal writing can be done in a number of ways (for example, by hand in a notebook, on a device such as a smartphone or tablet). However, the value of writing by hand cannot be underestimated, and we explore this in the next theme.

The link between writing and understanding

Writing is a skill and hence something that we learn and improve upon. As children most of us learned to read more quickly than we learned to write, and many students say that the most difficult things on their course are their written assignments. Writing often leads to a significantly deeper level of reflection than thinking alone, as it slows our thought processes down.

Writing gives us a much sharper focus and helps us to concentrate; it is almost impossible to write about something without thinking about what you are writing at the same time. So why is this the case? Research in neuroscience shows that writing by hand stimulates the reticular activating system (RAS) at the base of the human brain (Pérez Alonso, 2015). The RAS acts as a filter for information that the brain needs to process and ensures that we pay more attention to what we are actively focusing on at a given moment. Writing, therefore, sharpens our focus and is usually a more effective way of learning than discussion or reading. This means that you will be much more likely to remember something you have written down than something you have read or discussed; and, in addition, you have a record that you can refer back to. Having a sharp focus is one key aspect of carrying out a good research project.

Writing always involves making decisions about what to write, which means processing your thoughts and expressing yourself in words; this helps your understanding to develop. For example, when you take notes from reading a text, simply copying it will not help you to understand it, but summarising it and putting it into your own words probably will. In pieces of written work, you might need to explain the approach you have taken so that you or someone else can read it and understand what you have written. So, the act of writing helps us to develop our understanding.

However, we live in a world where most of us use some kind of keyboard more than we write by hand. In addition, most of us can type more quickly than we can write. So, do we need to write by hand? We know that writing by hand slows us down and helps us to remember things. An interesting study by Mueller and Oppenheimer (2014) showed that students who used laptops for taking their lecture notes produced poorer-quality work than those who took notes by hand. This is because those using laptops tended to try to type the lecturer's every word, while those who wrote by hand had to be much more selective about what they wrote. This forced them to begin processing the material straightaway; this is what helped them to perform better in their studies. So, writing by hand does seem to have some benefits. However, it is important to bear in mind that if you have a particular learning support need (for example, dyslexia) using a keyboard might be a much better option for you. So, remember, it's all about knowing what suits you best and not being afraid to experiment.

Try this

Think about the resources you will need for your research journal. What are your own particular preferences: handwritten or electronic? If you enjoy writing by hand, what kind of notebook might you find most helpful? Will you use other devices (for example, your tablet or smartphone) for some aspects? If so, which ones, and if not, why not? If you prefer using technology, which device will you use? Remember, there are no correct answers; it is all about how you learn best and finding what works for you. You could note down your thoughts in the space oppositite.

How to get started with reflective writing

Many of you will have done some reflective writing already on your course; for others this will be a new and different kind of writing. Reflective writing is generally more personal, and much of what you write in a research journal will be written in the first person. When I was struggling to write the methodology chapter of my doctoral thesis (I found out later that many students find this difficult), one of the most helpful things that an experienced supervisor said to me was 'Tell me the story of your research; what you did and why, and what you didn't do and why not'. Immediately the task felt doable, and I began to speak and write much more freely. Much of what I said and wrote was in the first person, because it was about my study. We know that it is rare for a research project to go completely to plan and that robust research considers issues of subjectivity. This means that being aware of our feelings during the 'ups' and 'downs' of the process and any assumptions we might be making will be important aspects of being critically reflective.

Many students who are new to reflective writing need to know how to start, and Bolton and Delderfield's (2018) guidance on this is invaluable. In it they encourage us at various points to do what they call 'the six minute write' and give us these pointers:

- Write whatever comes into your head.

- Don't worry about the order of what you write.

- Time yourself and write for six minutes without stopping.

- Don't stop to examine what you have written.

- Don't worry about spelling, punctuation, grammar and so on. You can correct this later if you need to.

- Give yourself permission to write anything.

- Remember, whatever you write, it can't be wrong – it's yours and it's private; no one else needs to read it.

When I have asked students to do a 'six minute write' as part of a session, I usually receive a range of responses in return. Some find it easy and are surprised by how much they can write in six minutes. Others struggle and 'dry up' before six minutes is over. However, most appreciate that it helps to get them started in the reflective writing process. Keeping going is important, and many find that it gets easier with practice.

Try this

Have a go at doing a 'six minute write'. Think about your research and, using the points on the previous page, write whatever is in your head. How easy or difficult did you find it? How useful was it for you?

A model for reflective writing

People who are new to reflective writing often find that a structure or framework helps them in the early stages. It helps them to make a start, and they will then discard it later as writing reflectively becomes easier. Mantell and Scragg (2019) offer a helpful structure for writing a reflective journal, which is based on three stages. Each stage has accompanying questions to encourage a deeper reflective approach, and I have adapted them for application to research.

Stage 1 – Reflecting

Here you focus on an issue or a concern that you have in relation to your research. Like Bolton and Delderfield (2018) Mantell and Scragg advocate free and spontaneous writing in order to capture your thoughts and feelings.

Stage 2 – Analyse

This is the most complex of the stages and involves responding to key questions:

- What is happening here?

- What assumptions am I making in relation to my research?

- What does this show about my beliefs (for example, my belief in my ability to carry out research, how the research process should run or what a good outcome would look like)?

Stage 3 – Action

The focus here is on the action you take following the analysis. Again, the authors suggest considering some key questions:

- What action can I take to move my research forward?

- How can I learn from what has happened so far in my research project?

- Would I do anything different if similar things occurred again?

- What does this experience tell me about my beliefs about myself, and my research capabilities?

While a model like this can be useful, there is no single correct way to write in a research journal. Here are two examples of extracts about reflective writing to illustrate this.

My supervisor says I need to keep a journal. What a pain! Some people seem to find this easy and I can see they've already written pages and pages of handwritten notes. It's early days but I've tried, and I just can't get the hang of it. I seem to get completely stuck and can't think of anything to write. Why is this so difficult? Today I'm going to try something different and use the notes app in my phone to see if that works any better.

Try this

Write your next journal entry and try using Mantell and Scragg's framework. Did it help? If so, why, and if not, why not?

What would I do without my notebook? I love it! I think I've always loved writing. It's such a great way to offload and de-stress. This project is definitely going to be stressful, so this journal will be like my best friend – listening to me, supporting me and never criticising or answering back! But hopefully it will help me to organise my thoughts too and give me a way of keeping on track.

More food for thought

Now think about the story of your research project. How did it start? How far have you come now? Why not start writing your story here.

Remember, there are no rights and wrongs; do what comes most easily and go from there.

Alex's journal 1

So, it looks like I need to give this reflective writing thing a go. I've never done it before but seems like it's worth a try. Some people say it's helped them a lot; others say they can't be bothered with the extra work. I'd love to do well and make everybody proud, so here goes.

It's early days and I'm going to try some different things to see what might work. That brilliant notebook I was given at a fair could come in handy. These notes are on my tablet, so that's a start. Seems like I often have my best ideas when I'm walking to the campus, so I think I'll also try recording myself on my phone. That means I won't forget things. There's such a lot to take in at the moment and hopefully all of this will help me to cope.

Notes

....

....

....

....

Things that can make reflective writing easier and enjoyable

It is widely recognised that learning is easier when it is enjoyable, and reflective writing is no exception to this. Many people enjoy journal writing and here are some pointers to help you to do so too:

- Nice quality stationery – this doesn't need to cost a lot and can be very satisfying to use. If you're going to get a notebook, consider getting one that will stand out in your bag or on your desk, as a reminder to write in it. Different-coloured pens and pencils can help you to organise your reflections (for example, red for literature, green for methodology) and make them easier to sift through later on. Sticky notes, stickers and reminders can all appeal to your creative or organisational side too.

- A dedicated space on your favourite device – keeping all your reflective writing together in one place will help you to see your progress over time. Don't be afraid to add pictures, photographs and diagrams as visual reminders.

- Finding a reflective space – this could be at home, or could also be your favourite seat in the coffee shop, your room or a study area in the library, or a sunny bench in the park or on campus. It doesn't really matter where it is, as long as you feel comfortable and look forward to going there.

- Treat yourself – having your favourite hot drink and snack while writing is bound to make it more enjoyable.

- Meet up with a friend – writing doesn't have to be a solitary activity, so why not meet up with a friend and write together, or meet up afterwards?

All of these approaches mean you will be well equipped to start compiling your research journal, so do add to it often. This need not take up a lot of your time; you can write anywhere, and you will be surprised how much you can achieve by writing for as little as 15 minutes.

Theme 2 — Making a good start

This section will:

- encourage you to think about what you hope to achieve by the time your research is finished;

- help you to understand more about research methods;

- consider the term 'criticality' and how it applies to your research;

- explore the importance of making the most of relevant networks;

- explain the importance of a good research question.

Theme 2.1

What are you ultimately hoping to achieve?

At the beginning of any large task, it is good to spend some time thinking about what you hope to achieve and what you would like your final outcome to be. Your first piece of independent research is likely to be the largest piece of academic work you have undertaken so far. Making a start on any large activity can be daunting and it is easy to be overwhelmed by it, particularly when it can make a significant difference to your overall results. Having a picture of what you hope to achieve can help you to make a positive start.

Starting any large task is often one of the most difficult things and here is one way that could help you to tackle the sense of inertia you might feel at the beginning of the process. When thinking about many aspects of our development, Covey (2004: 95) encourages us to, 'Begin with the end in mind' (Habit 2). He argues that everything is created twice – first at the psychological level in our minds and then at the practical level in our actual experience. Having a personal vision for the future focusing on the end result or outcome is one way of helping us begin to see things more clearly in the early stages.

At this point it is worth spending some time thinking about what you hope to achieve in the coming months as you embark upon your research study. Here are some questions to help you begin to think things through:

- What are your long-term goals for your research? Imagine you are logging into the portal (or using whatever method you use) to get your results; what do you hope it will say?

- What are you researching? Try and sum this up in a short sentence or two.

- Why are you researching this particular area? Again, try and write a short summary.

- What are you looking forward to most in doing your research?

- What are the key areas where you feel you need to develop in the area of research?

- What could hinder your progress? Can you identify any particular barriers?

- How could you overcome these barriers to your development?

Having a clear vision for your research will play a vital part in helping you to maintain a high level of motivation for your study. This vision will be particularly important at those times when you want to give up or wish it was all over. These feelings are common and are experienced by many students in your situation. Going back to your vision at these times will be particularly important as it will remind you why you are doing what you are doing, and that ultimately all the hard work will be worth it.

Notes

....

....

....

....

....

....

....

....

Try this

Building on your responses to the questions, think about your vision for your research and write a statement for it. This should include:

- what you are hoping to learn from carrying out your research;

- why you feel it is important;

- how it might help you in the future.

Remember to keep your language concise; effective vision statements are memorable because they are usually relatively short.

If you find it easier, why not draw a diagram or picture to illustrate your vision, or even find a photograph that could inspire you? You could always print it and put it here.

Starting the research process

Many students look forward to their independent study or dissertation because it gives them an opportunity to delve deeper into an area of interest that they have identified. Many courses require students to start with an introduction to research methods, which can sometimes feel like a 'necessary evil', as something you have to do before you can start making progress with your own study. Universities have protocols to ensure that research is done in a robust way, can stand up to scrutiny and is carried out ethically. These protocols often include the following:

- Sessions – either taught or made available on the Virtual Learning Environment (VLE) – on the whole research process. These help you to understand key theory. You will also cover other key aspects such as research ethics, confidentiality, gaining informed consent and subjectivity.

- Preparing a research proposal. This is an outline of what you are hoping to do, including your proposed research questions, the areas of literature that you will draw upon, some detail regarding how you intend to carry out the research and how you will deal with any ethical issues that could arise. Sometimes your proposal is submitted as a piece of assessed work.

- Submitting your proposal to an ethics review panel. Following the panel meeting, tutors and/or supervisors will offer feedback and give guidance on anything that needs to be amended. At this point you may be asked to submit some revisions to your proposal before going ahead with your research, particularly if there are any ethical issues that are apparent. It will be important to address these carefully and quickly, so you don't lose important time for carrying out your research project.

All of these steps are important in preparing you for the research process and will help you to carry out your research confidently and well. It is good to remember that your research proposal is a working document, one that you can re-visit as your study progresses. As such, it is worth keeping it to hand, so that you can refer to it easily and quickly. This could mean having a copy of it on your desktop, and on your phone or tablet. Don't be afraid to write notes on it during your study, as these could act as important reminders during the writing-up phase.

Space for your thoughts

Theme 2.3   Criticality

'Criticality' is a term that you will have become familiar with during your time at university and is often linked with skills such as analysis and evaluation. However, criticality is also a state of mind or an approach to academic work that takes nothing for granted and questions everything. So, instead of accepting something as a 'given' and describing it, criticality is about questioning it; often this is done by asking the question 'Why?' Small children with a thirst for knowledge and understanding are experts in this. At times they ask this question constantly, until their tired parent or carer says something like 'Because I say so!'

As well as having a deep level of curiosity, a critical mind is also aware of issues of context and examines similarities and differences between particular concepts in different contexts. For example, why is learning in one particular area of the curriculum more difficult for some people than others? Someone with a critical mind is aware of their strengths and weaknesses, understands how they think and critiques what they are learning as they are learning it.

Critical thinking lies at the heart of criticality, and during your time at university you will have become used to being ready to question everything, even those things you have previously accepted at face value (Eales-Reynolds et al, 2013). Depending on your specific area of study, there is rarely a single correct answer; even in scientific disciplines, single solutions to complex problems are difficult to find.

Practising criticality is vital in order to do well in your research, and at times you may well experience a tension between thinking and taking action. Thompson's (2012: 119) 'helicopter vision' is a helpful concept in relation to this. When a helicopter is flying at a high level, it gives us an overview of the landscape or terrain beneath it. It helps us to rise above a situation, hover over it and see the big picture. Equally, a helicopter also has the ability to descend to a specific place to see things more clearly. Criticality in research involves both of these things: seeing the big picture and the detail. The big picture will help us to keep our focus and the detail will show us where we need to take action. Criticality can help you to think creatively and innovatively as well; this is particularly important for gaining the highest marks according to university assessment criteria.

Notes

Criticality is an approach, therefore, that you will need to take throughout your research study. Your previous years of study at university should have prepared you well for this, but even so, don't forget that support is available to help you to do some 'fine tuning' in this particular area. This could be via your tutor or supervisor, or centrally in university support services (for example, the library).

Theme 2.4   Making the most of networks

Networks are important in many areas of life and studying is no exception. Carrying out your research study successfully will undoubtedly be easier when you have people around to support you. Having a supportive network will be particularly important during those times when your research doesn't go according to plan, or if you find yourself experiencing other difficulties, whether they are academic or personal. Here are a few suggestions of some key relationships you might want to foster in order to help you from the start:

- **Your supervisor** – building a good relationship with your supervisor cannot be over-emphasised, as we will see in Theme 7. Their support will be vital throughout your research study.

- **Your fellow students** – by now you may be part of a study group, which can offer invaluable support. If not, maybe now is a good time to think about forming one for the remainder of your programme. You might be involved in group supervision which could be just as effective.

- **Library staff** – most library staff are keen to help students with their research. Your research queries are often something more detailed and specific that they feel they can 'get their teeth into' so don't be afraid to ask for a small amount of their time. For example, some will be happy to offer a one-to-one session to help with your literature search. Some universities have subject librarians that specialise in a particular academic discipline, so find out if that is the case and seek out the relevant person.

- **Academic support staff** – many universities have staff who have a specific role in giving general academic support. They can help with such things as academic writing, checking references and proofreading. If you have them, do make use of them.

- **Your practical contacts** – if you are carrying out research that means you need to interview people or ask them to complete a survey, you may well need to build up some good relationships, so you have a range of people to ask. For example, if one person can't be interviewed during a particular period of time, you will then have someone else you can ask. If one group cannot complete a survey, another of your contacts might be able to help you.

- **Your friends and family** – these are people who can support us 'through thick and thin', especially at those times when things go wrong, or we feel like giving up. Taking a bit of time out to catch up with them will usually make us feel better and help us to keep going. These are likely to be the people you celebrate with when your studies are complete.

Building strong and effective networks can be an overlooked part of your research project and you may well want to remember some of these people when you write your acknowledgements at the end of the process.

Try this

Think about the people in your network and make a list of them. Are there any gaps, and, if so, how might you fill them?

Theme 2.5

The importance of your research question

All research projects need to have a small number of clearly defined research questions. You should devise them early in the research process and they will usually be included in your proposal. Devising research questions can be difficult, but they are key to the success of your study. Imagine you are going on a camping holiday where the only tents available are traditional canvas ones; first you have to erect tent poles by banging them into the earth with a mallet in order to make a frame. Then you can hang the canvas over the tent poles, securing it to the ground with tent pegs. Your research questions are just like those tent poles, in that they support the whole structure of your study.

So, what makes a good research question and how can you arrive at one? First, you need to think about what you are trying to find out; it might be something you have become curious about and now you want to find out more. Second, you need to phrase it as a question; this is your main or overarching research question. Now you need to break this down into two or three sub-questions which will help you to explore your main question in more depth. It is often effective if your final sub-question leads you into some conclusions or recommendations.

Here is an example to help you: let's say you are interested in finding out about why people decide to give up smoking. Your main or overarching question might be something like:

What factors influence people who decide to give up smoking?

Your sub-questions might be:

- When do people begin to think about giving up smoking?

- What makes them want to give up smoking?

- What support do they feel they need to succeed?

These research questions are strong because they are:

- **open** – they prompt a detailed response and cannot be answered with a simple 'yes' or 'no';

- **clear** – the language is concise and unambiguous;

- **focused** – they prompt a targeted study;

- **achievable** – they are not too ambitious;

- **detailed** – they open up the possibility for analysis;

- **not leading** – they do not predict any results.

By contrast, weak research questions are often:

- long and wordy;

- too broad for a small-scale study;

- predictive and show the views of the researcher from the outset;

- two or more questions in one, so too big and potentially confusing;

- explanatory, leading to work that is too descriptive.

White (2017) offers excellent advice on devising research questions, including working on them before devising your method and collecting any data, and being careful with each word.

Remember that in qualitative research your research questions can, and probably will, change during the process of your study as you begin to engage with the Research Triangle (see Figure 10 on page 158). Research rarely goes completely according to plan and participants do not necessarily say what we expect them to say, nor should they. So, amending your research questions is to be expected. In fact, in qualitative research if your questions remain the same, you need to ask yourself why, particularly if you are falling into the trap of simply seeing what you want to see instead of examining the evidence you have gathered.

Try this

Think about your research questions. Try devising your main research question and two or three sub-questions using the guidance on these pages.

More food for thought

When you get to the point where you have some initial research questions, why not discuss them with someone, for example a fellow student you trust or your supervisor. What new ideas did this discussion give you and how did it help you to make sure that your research questions are fit for purpose?

Alex's journal 2

I feel really passionate about this single-use plastic thing. It was that programme about the oceans that did it – the plastic is everywhere and I'll never forget the awful pictures of a whale's insides full of bottles and plastic bags. Just terrible. How have we got to this and what can we do about it? It's such a massive problem now, it's hard to see how it could get better.

So, what am I interested in finding out? Went back to my research questions today and not sure that they're quite right yet. Most of them are closed (for example, how many items of single-use plastic are people using?) and finding out the answers will be really difficult. So, I need to open these up. Some of the questions are open (for example, how can using less be encouraged?) which is better. But I definitely need to work on them some more. I think I've got too many as well. Makes me feel like my study is huge! I need to keep asking myself which aspect of this massive topic am I really interested in. Another topic to discuss with my flat mates tonight!

Top Tip

The importance of getting started

Getting started on a research project is often one of the most difficult things, and procrastination can easily set in for a number of reasons (see Theme 3). However, once we actually make a start, we usually feel better, so here are some suggestions to help you to get going.

- Visit the library and find at least one research methods book that you can engage with. Read it in whatever way helps you most (skimming, scanning, reading parts of it in depth) and take some notes on the key chapters.

- Carry out a very general literature search into your topic area. You could start with an internet search using a reliable scholarly search engine and be sure to make a note of key chapters and articles that you find.

- If you plan to carry out empirical research, start making relevant contacts so people will be well prepared once your proposal has been approved.

- Make use of any relevant sessions that are being offered in your faculty or by central services (for example, the library). Remember these are often available online too via your VLE, so are accessible at any time.

All of these things will help you to write your research proposal and will help you to feel like you are making a start.

Notes

....

....

....

....

....

....

....

Theme 3

Time management

This section will:

- help you to make a plan for your research;
- enable you to avoid the downsides of planning;
- prepare you to set some goals for your research;
- help you to deal with procrastination;
- examine ways to generate the required word count.

Theme 3.1

Making a research plan

Having a workable plan in place will be a key part of your success, and it is good to work on this early on in the research process, as it will help to give you a sense of purpose and direction. Keeping the final deadline in mind will be important; whatever happens, you will want to avoid incurring a penalty for submitting your work late without applying for extenuating circumstances. Doing this is simply not worth it.

Because your dissertation is a large piece of work, it is good to break it down into its component parts. In time management literature this is often referred to as the 'salami method' (Tracy, 2017; Bliss, 2018). As we know, a salami is a large sausage that is usually eaten in thin slices. Even people who love salami would find it very difficult to eat a whole one; and if they did they might well suffer the digestive consequences! Writing a good dissertation is generally not something that can be achieved in one go, so you will need to break it down to make it manageable. Using the salami method to do this kind of detailed planning can help you to start work in good time. Each step you take towards the deadline will help you feel that you are making progress.

Starting with the deadline date and working back from it is often a good way to begin the planning process. Then you need to work out how many weeks there are between now and that date. Working back from the submission date means you will be able to make a provisional plan of what you need to do and by when. Making a weekly plan often works well, as this breaks things down into manageable 'chunks'. Initially you could try using your dissertation guidance as an outline (for example, introduction, literature review, methodology, data analysis, discussion, conclusions) to map out what you will aim to do week by week. You also need to remember to include time to prepare for gathering your data (for example, devising interview questions or putting together a questionnaire) and carrying out a pilot study if relevant, followed by time for gathering the data. Remember to include attending relevant sessions on research methods in your plan, as well as supervision sessions, time for your literature search and independent reading, and for writing up. Working ahead of the deadline will be important in order to allow enough time for editing, making corrections and proofreading your work.

Notes

Try this

Try making an initial weekly plan for your research project. Think carefully about what you need to do and when. Remember that this is a working document that you will undoubtedly change as your study progresses.

Does planning always work?

While planning is generally seen as a positive thing, it is also good to be aware that planning can have its disadvantages, especially if you become a 'slave' to it. Planning can take up a lot of time, and it is easy to get caught in the trap of thinking that you must stick to your plan rigidly come what may. Two things are worth bearing in mind; first, because you carry out your study over quite a long period of time, your motivation is likely to fluctuate. At certain times you might feel more like doing particular aspects of the task rather than others. This means that at any given time you might not feel like doing whatever is on your plan. If you decide to stick to your plan, you may then not achieve as much and fall behind. If this continues, panic can set in; this can make you feel immobilised and unable to do anything.

At times like this it is often better to adopt a flexible approach to your plan and to do the things you are motivated to do, as you will probably make more progress. However, most of us like certain aspects more than others and it will be important to overcome the ever-present desire to procrastinate (see Theme 3.4), and to put off doing the difficult parts and the things you don't like. Be sure to build in plenty of time into your plan, so you can make changes to it at a later date if (or when) things do not go as you expect.

It is also good to think about where you will keep your plan so that you have it to hand. Your research journal is one obvious place, and, as we saw in Theme 1, this will be much more secure than having it on a piece of paper that you can easily lose (see Theme 1.2). You could also consider putting it on a large sheet of paper above your computer, as well as scanning it and sending it to your university email address and having it on your smartphone or tablet. That way you will always have a copy of it in case you lose it, and you'll always have it with you when you need to refer to it.

Occasionally students have said to me that planning does not help them; in fact, it hinders them. This can be the case for a number of reasons and some of them relate to a student's particular learning needs (for example, certain types of dyslexia). If this is the case for you, you will probably find it better to do what works for you. However, if your strategies stop working at any point, do remember to access the learning support that, hopefully, has been organised for you.

Space for your thoughts

Theme 3.3

Setting goals for your research

In many different areas of life having some clear goals helps us to achieve. You might be accustomed to setting goals, you might have intended to set them in the past and not done so, or the whole idea of goal-setting might still be quite new to you. However, if we don't know what we want to achieve, we won't have a sense of direction and purpose, and can then feel that we are not making progress.

Goals can be long term (for the duration of your study), medium term (for the next month) and short term (for the coming week). Many agree that goals need to be SMART:

- **Specific** – if they are too general, they may not be particularly useful in giving us a clear sense of direction or purpose. They need to contain a level of detail to be helpful.

- **Measurable** – we need to be able to measure the progress we are making towards them.

- **Achievable** – we need to know that we can achieve them. Setting goals that we are unlikely to achieve is very demotivating and can make us feel like giving up. But goals need to challenge us

too; if we can achieve them too easily, they may not stretch us.

- **Realistic** – we need to be honest with ourselves when setting goals; if we set goals that can only be achieved in an ideal world, we probably won't achieve them, which is very disheartening.

- **Time scaled** – deadlines are important reminders to keep our progress in check and help us with the constant battle against procrastination.

Table 1 provides examples that show how these principles can be applied to your research study.

Achieving SMART goals is a positive process because it raises our motivation, which encourages us to set more goals; this means we enter a positive cycle, which is often depicted as an upward-moving spiral. However, the spiral can also work in reverse if we set goals that are vague, general or unachievable; the result is that our motivation drops and we soon begin to think that we can't do it after all.

Table 1: Examples of helpful and less helpful goals

Helpful goals	Less helpful goals
Specific Devise ten questions for survey Carry out interview with first participant	Devise survey questions Carry out research interviews
Measurable Devise ten questions to discuss with supervisor Carry out and record interview	Prepare questionnaire Complete interviews
Achievable Allocate time to devise questions Schedule interview and send confirmation	Devise questions as and when Discuss interview time
Realistic Devise a small number of questions Identify one interview in the period of time	Devising questions only a small task Interviews should be enjoyable, quick and easy to do
Time scaled Arrange date for discussion of the ten questions with supervisor Set a date for completion of the interview	Lots of time to devise questions so to be done later Carry out research interviews

Try this

Try setting some SMART goals for your study. Remember, your long-term goal is set for you because you probably already have your submission date. So, think about your short- and medium-term goals, using the examples on the left-hand side of the table to help you.

Theme 3.4 — Dealing with procrastination

We can all experience the temptation to put things off, particularly when we have a significant length of time before something needs to be done. When a deadline is still far ahead, it is easy to be lulled into a false sense of security and think we have lots of time. As a result, we sit back and rest in the assurance that we will make progress later. This is procrastination and is often referred to as 'the thief of time'; time always moves on, so the result of putting things off is that the time we had is stolen from us.

There are many reasons why we procrastinate, and here are some of them:

- Nobody enjoys everything, and we tend to put off the things we don't like doing.

- Nobody is good at everything, and we tend to put off the things we find difficult.

- We can all get distracted by things that we find more interesting at the time and that grab our attention.

- We all get interrupted and feel we should respond to things quickly in our fast-paced world.

Dealing with procrastination will be important at every stage of your research study, and here are some things you can try:

- Focusing on what you enjoy is good, but putting off all the aspects you dislike is generally not to be recommended. Try doing small parts of these as you go along (the salami method again); that way you won't have to do all of them at once, and it will all feel more manageable.

- Focusing on your strengths is a good thing, but, again, leaving all the difficult parts to the end will mean a lot of very hard work later. For example, if you know you need to read a difficult text, or write a difficult section, break it down into smaller parts and do them one at a time. That way you will feel like you are making progress.

- You can often deal with distractions by removing them. If you know that you like to 'keep your eye' on particular things, only access them at particular times. For example, close down the relevant websites on your computer screen and turn off your mobile phone; you will be able to catch up later and you may well find it more enjoyable then.

- You can often deal with interruptions in this way too. If you know you are 'addicted' to email, turn it off; the same applies to social media. If you know that people knock on your door for a chat, find somewhere else to work (for example, in the library) where it will be more difficult to disturb you.

This does not mean isolating yourself. It will help you to keep a focus on your study and you might well find you enjoy your 'down time' more when you take time out to relax.

Try this

Think about the main reasons why you procrastinate. Make a list of these in the table provided, with reasons and possible ways of overcoming them. There is an example included to help you to make a start.

Table 2: Ensuring progress

What I put off doing	Reasons	How to overcome this
Reading relevant journal article	Difficult to understand	Read in four sections rather than all at once

Theme 3.5

Reaching a large word count

Any research project will almost certainly involve writing a longer piece of assessed work, perhaps even the longest piece you have written so far in your academic career. This can be daunting, and the salami method (see Theme 3.1) is very useful again here. Breaking the project down into its constituent parts is a very positive way of coping with the size of the task and can make it seem much more manageable. There are different ways in which things can be broken down and here are a couple of examples.

Many universities operate a system of asking students to write a certain number of words to gain a certain number of academic credits; typically, this is 4,000 words for a 20-credit module. Bear in mind that most dissertations or research projects attract 40 or even 60 credits, so the word count stipulated can often be 8,000 or 12,000 words. Obviously, this is significantly longer than you might be used to.

Some students cope by thinking of it in terms of writing two or three pieces of assessment for their modules rather than one long piece. This can make a real difference, and the work immediately becomes more doable because they have done it before and succeeded.

Another way of thinking about it is to break the work down by imposing a structure on it. Often this is given to you, at least in part, in the form of dissertation or project guidance. Adding a word count to each of the sections can help you see what you need to do more clearly while again making the task seem more achievable. As an example, I often speak to my own students about using the following as a general framework for an 8,000-word project:

Introduction 1,000 words

Literature review 2,000 words

Methodology 2,000 words

Data analysis and discussion 2,000 words

Conclusions 1,000 words

Some tutors prefer data analysis and discussion to be in separate sections, so if in doubt be sure to follow the advice given.

As you reach the point of writing up your findings, think about how you will manage the longer word count. Whatever method makes it seem achievable is well worth implementing.

Space for your thoughts

....
....
....
....
....
....
....
....
....
....

More food for thought

As well as breaking large things down into their component parts, it is also good to spend a bit of time thinking about the whole project. Using the headings in Theme 3.5 (or your project guidance if this is different), take a bit of time to map out section by section how you will write up your study. Include the number of words you need to write and some headings regarding the content you will want to include.

Alex's journal 3

I've always been terrible at time management and having this big project to manage really scares me. I've got loads of time but I can't believe how quickly it goes. We're two weeks in already. Exams are looming as well and I'll need lots of time to revise. I'm enjoying my project and feel I'm learning loads about single–use plastic. Sometimes though it feels like the whole thing is just enormous, and I'll be really glad when it's done.

Feels like I should at least try and make a plan this time even if I don't stick to it. Thinking about all I've got to do makes me feel stressed out and I want to bury my head in the sand. There's so much riding on this it makes me panic a bit. But people seem to say doing a plan makes them feel better – really hope they're right! There's only one way to tell ...

Notes

....

....

....

....

Top Tip

'Don't get it right, get it written!'

During the final stages of writing my doctoral thesis, one of the supervisors said, 'Don't get it right, get it written!' This proved to be some of the best advice I had been given during the whole research process. As students we all want to 'get it right' and nobody wants to submit a research study that is weak or that might fail. However, if we are not careful, a desire to do well can also really hold us back.

So, what do we do if we feel this might be happening? The first thing is to face it head on; ignoring it, or simply hoping everything will be better tomorrow could well be like burying your head in the sand. You could try these ideas:

- **Be sure to speak to somebody** – for example, your supervisor or personal tutor or someone in central services (for example, in academic support). The phrase 'A trouble shared is a trouble halved' is often accurate, and simply talking about it can be the start of the process of getting yourself back on track.

- **Write something** – remember that writing helps our understanding, so write something related to your research project. Sometimes it does not matter what you write, as it can help to unblock your thoughts. You will then have something to work on, and it can be refined later.

- **Do something that you find easy** – for example, reading a clear text or writing a section that is more straightforward. Often this will help you 'get back into gear' and start achieving again.

- **Take a break** – sometimes we try to work when we are simply too tired; then everything takes longer and seems much more difficult.

It is good to resist the thought that we need to get it right first time, so don't be afraid to work on a first draft, ask someone for feedback and then go back to develop it. It will all be worth it in the end.

Theme 4

Reading for research

This section will:

- help you to decide what to read;
- enable you to target your reading successfully;
- explain the importance of a balanced reference list;
- help you to recognise when to stop reading;
- discuss how to keep a record of what you have read.

Theme 4.1

Deciding what to read

In Theme 2.5 we examined the importance of your research questions as things that support the whole of the research process. When undertaking any piece of research, everyone is faced with questions regarding what they should read, and having clear research questions can be very helpful here. In order to focus your reading, you need to pose the following question: what has been published already in relation to my research questions? This should give you some clear pointers in relation to topic areas for starting a literature search (Coughlan and Cronin, 2016).

For example, if you go back to the research questions on pages 34–35 in relation to a study on giving up smoking, an initial search via a scholarly source on the internet will point to some possible topic areas. These are just some of them, and there are more:

- health issues (for example, the greater likelihood of heart attack or stroke);

- 'buddy' systems to help people who want to give up smoking;

- smoking cessation interventions;

- trends in mortality rates;

- how to motivate people who want to give up smoking;

- women who give up smoking;

- young women in disadvantaged circumstances who give up smoking.

Making a list like this following an initial internet search in relation to your own research questions will help you in several ways. It will give you an impetus to start reading, and at this point it can be useful to do some skim reading to explore your research interests further. Even at this early stage it is good to keep some kind of record of what you have found, as finding it later might prove difficult and time consuming.

A search like this might help you to focus in on more specific aspects of your study (for example, health issues), or on a particular social group (for example, young women), and could sharpen the focus of your study, giving you Thompson's (2012) helicopter vision (see Theme 2.3). A study with a sharp focus is much easier to manage than a wide-ranging one, so this can be a very positive step forward.

A general search will help you to see the range of sources you might need to use (for example, academic texts, journal articles, research reports, government policy documents, newspaper articles). Most importantly it will give you a sense of a starting point and if you are genuinely interested in the area you are planning to research, it should act as a good motivator to your reading.

After carrying out this kind of activity, you may well find that you need to adjust your research questions as you engage with the Research Triangle depicted in Figure 10 on page 158. It is worth looking at this now if you haven't done so already.

For a range of good reasons, some students carry out a literature review as their whole research project; if this is what you are doing, it is well worth reading research methods literature on this specifically (Oliver, 2012). There are some good general sources that cover a range of academic disciplines and those that are discipline-specific; examples include Ridley (2012); Booth et al (2016); Aveyard (2018).

Try this

Go back to your research questions and ask yourself the question 'What has been published already in relation to these?' Now start to write a list of the topic areas that you will need to explore. Don't forget that you will also need to include literature on research methods (see Theme 5).

Notes

Theme 4.2

Targeting your reading

As part of your research project you will need to target what you read in order to make significant progress and to avoid feeling overwhelmed. Most people do a research study because they are interested in finding out more about a particular area. This makes reading about it enjoyable, but equally, it is very easy to get 'sidetracked' and read more than you need to. This is not a problem per se, but it can take up valuable time that you might need for other important aspects of your study.

By completing the previous activity, you have already taken the first step towards targeting your reading. You can now start to break down your list of topic areas into smaller parts by working on a more detailed list of specific things you feel you need to read by carrying out a literature search. A good place to start doing this is your university library catalogue (sometimes called LibrarySearch) and searching under your topic areas. Be sure to search in all areas (for example, books, ebooks, journal articles) to capture a wide range of resources. It is a good idea to list them all initially because from there you will be able to identify which are essential (those things

you must read) and which are desirable (those you can read if you have time); this will help you to plan your time further. Otherwise it is very easy to start reading things you are interested in only to find more important things later when you have already used up quite a lot of the time available to you.

Be sure to note down as much detail as you can in your list. For example, instead of just the title of a book, which particular chapter or chapters will you need to read? Reading the abstract of a journal article will help you to decide whether or not you need to read the whole thing. This is a very worthwhile thing to do at this point, as it may well eliminate things you think you need to read, but actually don't.

Doing a literature search for the first time is not necessarily easy and it is good to seek support if you feel you need it. There may well be relevant sessions on offer in your library, and if so, do take advantage of them. In addition, library staff will often be happy to help individual students when they ask for a short session. Don't forget your subject librarian who will undoubtedly be a very useful source of valuable information.

Think about how you can target your reading and start a more detailed list of what you need to read in relation to your topic areas. Use the table provided for your notes; in the right-hand column E/D stands for Essential or Desirable, and an example relating to research methods literature is included to help you get started.

Table 3: Priority reading

Source*	Location where found**	Reason	Detail stored	E/D
Punch (2014) Intro to social research	Library	Good resource mentioned by supervisor	Ethics chapter scanned and saved on laptop	E

* For example, title of book, journal article   ** For example, library, web address

Working towards a strong reference list

Many students ask how many references should be in a good reference list for a dissertation. This is a difficult question to answer and will depend on the length of the dissertation but, as a general guide, a strong reference list at undergraduate level will usually span at least two to three pages; at postgraduate level it will often be longer. But it is not only the number of references that matters, but the quality and range that is important too.

Depending on the subject area and academic discipline, a strong reference list for a dissertation or research study will often include:

- key textbooks

- other academic books

- chapters written by different authors in edited collections

- academic journal articles

- articles from professional journals

- pieces from reputable websites (for example, professional bodies)

- research reports from studies into your chosen area

- grey literature that is not produced by commercial publishers, which could include government reports and policy documents as well as unpublished work and conference proceedings

A strong reference list will also contain work that is current; as a general rule this is work that has been published within the last five years. Any list that does not contain any literature like this will be seen as dated, so having one or two items from this year or last will make your list look very up to date. When referring to academic books, always be sure to use the latest edition, as again, this will make your list look current.

However, in this particular aspect you need to beware of two things; first, don't assume that the latest version contains exactly the same things as the previous one. It is a new edition for a reason and the parts you wish to refer to may have changed as the author's ideas have developed over time. Second, it might be that the earlier edition contains more of what you need to refer to than the newer one; don't be afraid to make this point when writing up your literature review as this shows criticality and an eye for detail. You will then need to include both editions in your reference list.

A strong reference list also includes all seminal work in a given area. These are publications that have stood the test of time and are still relevant even though they were published some years ago. These will be specific to your topic area, and your reference list is likely to look incomplete without them.

You will know from previous experience that devising a strong reference list takes time and requires some careful attention to detail. It is a good idea to formulate it as you go along, rather than leaving it until the end, and using some of the tips in Themes 4.5 and 10.5 should help.

Knowing when to stop reading

Many students ask me, 'When do I know it's time to stop reading?' This can be difficult, but here are some possible indicators:

- When you start to read things you have read before in different sources; this is the point when you feel you are reading the same kinds of things about a topic area but written by different people. You may well find yourself thinking something like 'I've read that before' or 'X says that in their article on this subject'. If this happens several times, it is probably time to stop reading.

- When you feel like you are using reading as an excuse for procrastination, particularly if this is a way of putting off writing or collecting data. If you know that you should be doing something different and are being distracted by reading, again it could be time to stop, or at least time to do something different. Sometimes, it is too easy to use reading as an excuse for delaying other things that might be less interesting or more challenging. Equally, you might be a person who either always feels they need to read more, or they have never read

enough. Don't be afraid to use the length of your reference list as an indicator of how much you have read so far and act accordingly.

- When your list of references is becoming too long; universities vary as to whether or not the reference list counts in the overall word count. There is such a thing as a reference list that is too long; it could mean you are over-citing so your work will appear smothered in references. This means that your in-text references and your reference list will simply take up too many words in your word count.

- When the deadline is looming; this is bound to happen with the passage of time, and at this point your main emphasis will need to switch from reading to writing as it gets nearer.

A strong literature review is an important part of any dissertation, but remember it is only one part of it and, as such, it will only ever get you a certain percentage of the overall mark. A balanced study is the overall aim, so be sure not to neglect other important aspects by reading too much.

Space for your thoughts

Keeping a record of what you have read

Having a clear record of your reading is an important organisational aspect of any study, and doing this in an ongoing way is likely to save you lots of time later on. It is very frustrating and time-wasting to find that you can remember something important that you have read but can't find the details when you need them. Often this happens close to the deadline and at the time when you can least afford it, so here are some tips to help you to avoid this:

- Keep a record from the very beginning of your study; if you haven't done this yet, the time to start is now and using Table 3 on page 57 should help. The longer you leave it, the more difficult it will be. It might take some time, but it will definitely be worth it.

- Start your reference list now; there are so many benefits to doing this that it is hard to think of any drawbacks. Once you get into this habit, it will become easier and save you a huge chore later. You will undoubtedly be very pleased that you did this!

- Consider using a referencing tool if you haven't used one before; if your university

recommends a particular tool, it's always a good place to start. Some of the most common ones are RefWorks, EndNote, Zotero and Mendeley but there are others. Remember, some tools are much better than others, so always check the accuracy of any tool with a few examples before deciding whether or not to use it. Don't forget that Microsoft Word has a referencing tool under the Referencing tab which can help too.

- Keep a card index; this might sound old-fashioned, but some people find it easier.

- If you're not sure whether you will need a particular source, scan relevant documents on one of your university's multi-functional devices (MFDs) to your university email account; this is free to use and is cheaper and more environmentally friendly than photocopying. Save the files to your computer and label them clearly so you can see quickly what they are later. This means you are less likely to have to trawl through lots of files to find what you are looking for at that point in time. You might want to consider scanning:

» chapters from key books, particularly if they are popular and likely to be recalled if you loan them;

» journal articles;

» the cover of a book and the copyright page that gives you all the details for your reference list;

» a page of a book or article that contains a direct quote you want to use, because this will give you an important record of the page number that you will need to cite.

Keeping an accurate record of what you have read is a key aspect of the management of any study. It takes time, but it will be worth it.

Try this

Think about how you will keep a record of what you have read. Refer back to Table 3 on page 57 and start your record now, if you haven't already.

More food for thought

Now think about devising a mini reading list. Here are some headings you could use, but feel free to add your own and to remove some if they are not applicable to you.

- your favourite research methods books – these are books that explain the research process clearly and that you find easy to understand (for example, Denscombe, 2017; Thomas, 2017; Bell and Waters, 2018). Equally they might include larger textbooks on research methods such as Balnaves and Caputi (2001); Bryman (2016); Cohen et al (2017); Denzin and Lincoln (2017);

- academic texts that relate to your particular topic (for example, books, book chapters in edited collections, journal articles);

- grey literature from reputable websites, newspapers, magazines and other online sources.

Alex's journal 4

I've always loved reading and am really enjoying looking into this whole thing of single-use plastic. There is so much that's interesting and some that's a bit shocking. Even when I'm shopping I'm looking in people's trolleys and have to stop myself from stopping them and pointing out how much they're using!

But finding really good academic sources isn't that easy. It's really easy to find articles in newspapers and magazines and things on TV, but I know I need more than that. I'm not sure which way to go with this. Think I need to talk to my supervisor and people in the library as soon as I can. Hopefully they will be able to give me some pointers.

Case Study

Accessing the right support

Winston has dyslexia and is finding his dissertation very challenging. He always expected it to be difficult, but now feels he is really struggling. He has always been quite a slow reader and he is worried about falling behind. It is hard to concentrate for any length of time, and the literature review is proving particularly difficult.

Winston's dyslexia was diagnosed during his first year and until recently he has had a lot of contact with his specialist tutor. He felt he was progressing well, so he stopped contacting her. Winston decides to get in touch with the tutor again, and she is pleased to hear from him. They decide to meet, and she offers Winston some helpful support with organising what he needs to read and they discuss some strategies to help him succeed. In addition, she offers to proofread his work; together they set some deadlines for him to send sections of his work to her so she has a good amount of time to look at it. Winston is pleased that he didn't try to keep going on his own.

Notes

....

....

....

....

....

....

....

....

Theme 5

Key research terminology

This section will:

- help you to understand the term 'methodology';
- examine the links between methodology, epistemology and ontology;
- help you to understand quantitative and qualitative methods and when to use them;
- examine the terms 'reliability', 'validity' and 'generalisability' in research;
- help you to consider a range of research methods that are relevant for your study.

Theme 5.1

What does 'methodology' mean?

'Methodology' is a term that is not clearly defined and is best understood as an umbrella term for a system, in this case a system for researching a particular area. Any methodology has a strong theoretical underpinning and as such provides a rigorous explanation of how we carried out a study and why we chose to do it in a particular way. At the risk of oversimplifying things, methodology is often embedded in two key paradigms (or groups of theories), depending on the philosophical stance taken in a particular study. These two paradigms are positivism and interpretivism and these can be seen as two ends of a spectrum as depicted in Figure 1.

We will continue to develop this figure as we progress through this theme to build what can be described as a hierarchy of objectives. A hierarchy of objectives is a tool that enables the analysis of a project in a step-by-step, or level-by-level, way.

Figure 1: Positivism and interpretivism

Positivist	Methodological paradigm	Interpretivist
Universal laws		No universal laws
Solution		Recommendations
Answer		Insights
What happens		Why things happen
Descriptions		Reasons
Explain		Explore

On the left-hand side of the figure, positivism argues that we research things to prove them through scientific enquiry. A very simple example here is that every time two atoms of hydrogen are put together with one atom of oxygen, you get water. It happens every time, can be done on any number of occasions with the same result and can be proved through the application of science. Positivists tend to look for universal laws based on a hypothesis.

Interpretivists, on the right-hand side of the figure, assert that in the social sciences things are often not as straightforward as in the earlier example; indeed, science is often not that straightforward either! When it comes to studying people, things are much less predictable. If we go back to our study on giving up smoking in Theme 2.5, it is easy to imagine that different research participants will respond in different ways, and therefore there will be no single correct answer or solution. The responses of participants will need to be interpreted to examine any new insights the study might bring; hence the term 'interpretivist' on the right-hand side of the figure.

However, not all social scientists use an interpretivist methodology. Those who want to generate descriptions of what happens (for example, which people have the greatest success rate in giving up smoking) will take a positivist approach to find out such things as the optimum age when this happens, and the length of time people have been involved in smoking. Those who want to find out why some people have more success than others will adopt an interpretivist methodology to discover such things as what motivates people to give up smoking. One easy way of remembering the distinction between positivist and interpretivist methodologies is that positivists tend to focus on what happens and interpretivists on how and why things happen; in short, positivists explain and interpretivists explore.

Try this

In general, it helps to think of methodology as a set of broad principles or rules governing how a piece of research is carried out. Think about your own research; is its methodology positivist or interpretivist, and why? Now write some notes.

The links between methodology, and epistemology and ontology

Having discussed methodology as a system for carrying out research, two other 'ologies' come to the fore: epistemology and ontology. In fact, we have already covered some aspects of these in Theme 5.1, so we will refer back to them here.

'Epistemology' is a term used to describe knowledge, and in particular how we know what we know. As discussed in Theme 5.1, this will be either through the application of science (positivism) or through the interpretation of data (interpretivist). Epistemology is, therefore, the theory of knowledge that underpins any research study. Going back to Theme 5.1, a study that seeks to find answers to a hypothesis through the application of science (for example, which people have the greatest success rate in giving up smoking) will have a positivist epistemology. A study that seeks to explore why people do certain things (for example, what motivates people to give up smoking) will have an interpretivist epistemology. These terms have been added in Figure 2 in order to build the hierarchy of objectives further.

In your readings about methodology, another 'ology' you will come across is

'ontology'; again, we covered this in part in Theme 5.1. Ontology refers to the view of reality we adopt and again can fall on either end of our spectrum. If we have a single view of reality and believe that there is one answer or a clear solution, we will adopt a positivist ontology (for example, a study that seeks to find the greatest success rate in giving up smoking). However, if we know that there will be a range of answers or insights that emerge from our study, we will adopt an interpretivist ontology (for example one that explores what motivates people to give up smoking). These terms have been added in Figure 3.

Other technical terms that are often added to this particular mix are 'objectivist' and 'subjectivist'. Generally, the term 'objective' relates to something that is factual, and 'subjective' to something based on opinion. So, in our examples the first study could be said to have a positivist objectivist epistemology while the second has an interpretivist subjectivist epistemology. These are great words to use when writing the methodology section of your dissertation! These terms have been added in Figure 4 in order to build the hierarchy of objectives further.

Figure 2: Theories of knowledge

Epistemology	Theory of knowledge underpinning the study	Epistemology
Appliance of science		Interpretation of data

Figure 3: Theories of reality

Ontology	The view of reality adopted in the study	Ontology
One single reality One solution One correct answer		Multiple realities A number of solutions Multiple answers

Figure 4: Methodological viewpoint

Objectivist	The view of reality adopted in the study	Subjectivist
Factual Provable		Opinion Cannot be proved

Quantitative and qualitative method

The term 'method' is used to describe how research is carried out, and the method you choose for your study depends on what you want to find out. It is sometimes used to mean 'methodology' and vice versa; this can be very confusing. In general, there are two main types of method, and these are as follows:

- **Quantitative** – explains things by collecting numerical data and using mathematical approaches (or statistics). This is the easier of the two terms to explain because it always involves numbers; if there are no numbers in your study, you are not employing a quantitative method.

Taking our example of the study into giving up smoking further, finding out how many people are successful in a given period will involve collecting numerical data and presenting it in order to reach some conclusions. So, this study employs a quantitative method.

But even things that are not numerical in nature can be examined using quantitative method (for example, in a survey; see Theme 5.5).

- **Qualitative** – explores things by collecting verbal data that is then analysed and interpreted. In effect, it is any kind of research that does not involve numerical data, and while it often involves the use of language and words, it can also include such things as observations, and the use of pictures or photographs.

In our study into what motivates people to stop smoking, a qualitative method could gather verbal data (for example, from interviews), and it could also involve presenting participants with a number of anti-smoking photographs or slogans and asking for their responses.

As discussed previously, whether you decide to use a quantitative or qualitative method in your study will depend on what you want to find out. Each method has advantages and disadvantages, and some of these are summarised in Table 4.

Whatever method you select, it is useful to remember that a discussion of the points in the table gives your methodology section a higher level of critique than simply describing what you did.

Figure 5: Main differences between quantitative and qualitative method

Quantitative	Qualitative
Explains phenomena – can give a clear picture of what is happening	Explores phenomena – can give some insights into what is happening and why
Aims at drawing objective conclusions	Is interested in subjective meanings
Can only say what happens and not why	Can offer reasons why things happen
Offers descriptions which can be relatively shallow	Offers more in-depth descriptions of what is taking place
Can offer more generalisability (see Theme 5.4)	Offers transferability and trustworthiness

Table 4: Comparison of quantitative and qualitative method

Quantitative	Method	Qualitative
Numerical data Explains objective descriptions		Verbal data Explores subjective reasons

Try this

Many researchers choose either a quantitative or qualitative method; however, some choose to combine the two and take a mixed method approach (Creswell and Creswell, 2018). For example, some choose to look at the bigger picture using the quantitative method and then to explore an aspect related to their study using the qualitative method. However, a mixed method approach will often involve significantly more work, and keeping your study to a manageable size is always a good thing. Now think about your own method. Is it quantitative, qualitative or a mixture of both? Give some reasons why you plan to carry out your research in this way.

Validity, reliability and generalisability in research

In all research it is important to consider issues of validity and reliability carefully to ensure that a study is robust, can stand up to some level of scrutiny and is, thereby, of good quality. This means you need a clear understanding of the terms themselves, and posing these two questions can help you in this regard:

- **Validity** – is the research measuring what it is meant to measure, or exploring what it is meant to explore?

- **Reliability** – if this research were carried out again in similar circumstances, would the results be approximately the same?

Heale and Twycross (2015: 66) give a simple but memorable example here: 'An alarm clock rings at 7 am each morning but is set for 6.30 am. It is reliable (it consistently rings at the same time each day) but is not valid (because it is not ringing at the time set).'

Validity and reliability are important for all research and are often easier to measure in a quantitative study. In a qualitative study both terms can present particular challenges because there is no agreement on how they should be measured, or indeed if they can

be measured. In general, these terms are applied to the researcher rather than the study in this way. Validity in qualitative research often refers to the integrity of the researcher, how they explain their own position in the research (see Theme 6.2), how they have applied the method chosen and the accuracy involved in presenting the data. Reliability in qualitative research relates to the level of consistency employed in data analysis (Noble and Smith, 2015).

The term 'generalisability' is linked with both validity and reliability, and considers whether the findings from a research study could be applied in other similar circumstances or situations. In qualitative research, the term 'generalisability' is often replaced by the terms 'transferability' and 'trustworthiness' and refers to the researcher providing sufficient evidence to show that the findings could be applied to other situations. This is often achieved by writing thick descriptions (Korstjens and Moser, 2018).

In a small-scale study, claims of generalisability and transferability need to be stated tentatively (for example, in your conclusions), otherwise they might not stand up to scrutiny. In the example in Theme 2.5, making bold claims of generalisability would be unwise, because even if it appears that people in certain age groups have greater success in giving up smoking in this particular sample, that may not always be the case. Similarly, the motivation for giving up smoking can vary between people, be relatively individual and not necessarily be applicable to others.

Research methods

Research methods are sometimes referred to as research instruments, and they are the tools used by researchers to carry out a study. The most common methods used are as follows:

- **surveys**, often carried out using a questionnaire – these can be quantitative if asking for yes/no answers, or using Likert scales (for example, on a scale of 1–10 how likely are you to give up smoking this year, 1 being very unlikely and 10 being very likely?), or qualitative if asking open questions (for example, what did you find difficult about giving up smoking?);

- **interviews** – qualitative;

- **focus groups** – qualitative;

- **observations** – can be quantitative (for example, counting the number of times people expressed their intention to give up smoking) or qualitative (for example recording how people intend to give up smoking).

Research methods are shown in Figure 6, adding to our hierarchy of objectives.

Some students at undergraduate level undertake empirical research, where they collect evidence by using one or more of the methods listed here. Others carry out desk research, sometimes called secondary research, while others do a literature review; Master's-level students sometimes do this too. Secondary research often involves the analysis of data collected previously, for example from a published study, or from a data source that is accessible to them. It can also involve the analysis of a documentary or film. This kind of research can give you an opportunity to study something in depth where access to data is difficult (a common example here is a study of suicide, where contacting people could cause harm), and can be a useful backup if your study does not go according to plan (see Theme 8.2). In these instances, desk research offers a good reliable alternative.

Try this

Think about the research methods you plan to use and why; make some notes on your thoughts here.

Figure 6: Research methods

Research methods	Methods	Research methods
Survey Questionnaire Observation		Interview Focus group

Notes

....

....

....

....

....

....

....

....

....

....

More food for thought

At some point it's probably worth doing two things to help you to continue thinking about how your understanding of your research is developing.

- Go back to the literature from your research methods module. Is there anything here that is useful that you have overlooked?

- Go back to your research proposal. Have things changed? If so, why, and if not, why not?

Alex's journal 5

All this methodology stuff is really doing my head in. It's a minefield. I've asked my tutor to explain it and I still don't get it — I can't ask again! Everybody I ask doesn't seem to understand it either, so I guess I'm not alone. I've looked at loads of definitions and they all seem to say something slightly different — so frustrating! How can they expect us to write about it when there's not even one clear definition we can use? Some people seem to have decided just to leave it out, but that seems like a bad idea to me. To start with I'm going to have a go at writing a description of what I did and see if I can go from there. Maybe the writing of it will help me to understand it — I definitely don't understand it at the moment, that's for sure! If I don't do this, I know I'll put it off and it will get worse. If I'm feeling brave enough, maybe I'll take what I've written to my next supervision session and show it to my supervisor ...

Space for your thoughts

Top Tip

A hierarchy of objectives

During a supervision session a supervisor said to me, 'Think of your methodology section as a hierarchy of objectives, where you can track your study from top to bottom, or from bottom to top, starting at any point.' At this point I was struggling to write this particular section and decided to write it using three headings – first, 'methodology', then 'method' and finally 'methods'. This really helped me to understand what I needed to write.

In Theme 5.1 a hierarchy of objectives was described as a tool that enables the analysis of a project in a step-by-step, or level-by-level, way. In Figure 7 all the previous figures from this section have been put together to form a hierarchy of objectives with bi-directional arrows linking each of the levels.

Using the example from Theme 2.5 again here, and following the arrows on the left-hand side of the figure from the bottom to the top, a study that seeks to describe who has the most success in giving up smoking (for example,

age group or gender) could be done through the use of a questionnaire, which would be a quantitative method with an objectivist ontology and epistemology, employing a positivist methodology.

By contrast, on the right-hand side, a study that seeks to explore people's motivation for giving up smoking could be done by carrying out a number of interviews, which would be a qualitative method with a subjectivist ontology and epistemology, employing an interpretivist methodology.

When writing your methodology section, you may prefer to use the hierarchy of objectives from the bottom to the top to describe how you carried out your study rather than from top to bottom – it's up to you. In addition, if you examine what you didn't do and why, your methodology section will probably be more analytical and will enable you to show a wider understanding of research methods in general.

Figure 7: A hierachy of objectives

Positivist	Methodological paradigm	Interpretivist
Universal laws Solution Answer What happens Descriptions Explain		No universal laws Recommendations Insights Why things happen Reasons Explore

⇕   ⇕

Epistemology	Theory of knowledge underpinning the study	Epistemology
Appliance of science		Interpretation of data

⇕   ⇕

Ontology	The view of reality adopted in the study	Ontology
One single reality One solution One correct answer		Multiple realities A number of solutions Multiple answers

⇕   ⇕

Objectivist	The view of reality adopted in the study	Subjectivist
Factual Provable		Opinion Cannot be proved

⇕   ⇕

Quantitative	Method	Qualitative
Numerical data Explains objective descriptions		Verbal data Explores subjective reasons

⇕   ⇕

Research methods	Methods	Research methods
Survey Questionnaire Observation		Interview Focus group

Theme 6

Research ethics

This section will:

- discuss the term 'ethics' in relation to research;
- help you to understand more about ethical issues in research;
- enable you to consider how to deal with issues of subjectivity and avoid making assumptions;
- outline some ideas for maintaining confidentiality and protecting your data;
- help you to think about how to gain informed consent from your participants.

Theme 6.1

What are ethics?

Ethics can be defined simply as norms for behaviour and involve being able to distinguish between acceptable and unacceptable ways of doing things. This also applies to research, and carrying out research in an ethical way is always important. Beauchamp and Childress (2013) first published their seminal work on biomedical ethics in 1979 where they outlined four key principles to ethical practice. These are:

- **autonomy** – people have the right to make their own decisions, and this should be respected;

- **non-maleficence** – do no harm;

- **beneficence** – do good;

- **justice** – the greatest good for the greatest number.

These principles have been applied in many different professional fields and, while all four principles can be applied to research, the first two in particular warrant some careful attention. Autonomy means that research participants have the right to decide for themselves whether or not they wish to take part in a study, and they should

not be coerced or pressured in any way. Non-maleficence is especially important, as research should not cause any harm to participants or affect them adversely. Ethical research respects human dignity and privacy; it is good to remember that research participants give their information freely and voluntarily and we should always handle it with respect and care.

That your research is carried out in an ethical way is ensured through university processes. If you are undertaking an empirical study, you will be asked to present a proposal to your ethics committee; this is often done as part of the process of writing your research proposal.

Once your proposal has been examined by the committee you might be asked to make some changes to it because of possible ethical issues. This safeguards you as the researcher and your participants; you will need to make any necessary changes and have them approved before starting to gather your data. This doesn't apply if you are planning a piece of desk research or a literature review, and both can be good ways of dealing with ethical issues that might otherwise be unavoidable.

Space for your thoughts

Some common ethical issues in empirical research

Theme 6.2

There are some common ethical issues that researchers face when carrying out empirical studies with human participants which we will now consider (Oliver, 2010). Many of these involve respect – a general term that is often taken to mean acting with due attention to the feelings, wishes and rights of others:

- **Honesty** – whatever data we gather must be represented honestly and accurately. In research we do not always hear what we expect to hear (nor should we: see Theme 2.5), and we need to be true to the data we have gathered; this means not adjusting data to fit with what we were hoping or expecting to find and not misrepresenting them in any way.

- **Confidentiality** – any information shared by participants (whether through an interview, a questionnaire or an observation) is gathered for use in the study only and needs to be treated with care. This area is covered in more detail in Theme 6.4.

- **Consent** – all participants need to give their permission for the data they are sharing to be used. They should also have the right to withdraw from a study at

any point if they decide they no longer wish to participate. How to do this effectively is discussed in Theme 6.5.

While all of these issues need to be considered, if a study involves participants who are considered to be vulnerable in any way, extra care will need to be taken, including being sure they have access to support, should it be needed.

At this point it is also good to begin to consider the area of subjectivity (see Theme 6.3). To some extent, all research is subjective because we all have beliefs and personal values that we apply to people and situations (Denzin and Lincoln, 2017).

Reflexivity in research is defined as the ability to see those things that are influencing our thoughts, behaviours and actions (Fook and Askeland, 2006) and as such involves a high level of self-awareness and a deep level of critical reflection. Reflexivity acts as a safeguard against assumptions and, particularly in qualitative research, will involve being clear about where we stand on key aspects of our research. This is often referred to as positionality (Finley, 2008) which argues that all knowledge is culturally situated and is thereby influenced by social context.

Try this

Think about any ethical issues you might
face when carrying out your research.
If you are doing desk research, or a
literature review, which ethical issues
will you avoid? Kara (2018) argues
that doing this kind of research ethically
means being sure to present someone
else's research accurately, particularly
in relation to its context, so as not to
misrepresent it in any way. How can you
be sure that you are doing this?

Having a strong interest in a particular area is important for any researcher's motivation, but this also means that researchers are likely to have formed some opinions about aspects of the subject before the study even begins. These opinions could well be based on some assumptions, which could subsequently lead to criticisms of subjectivity and even bias. This is something that all researchers need to beware of, and an understanding of how assumptions are made can be helpful in making sure that a piece of research will stand up to scrutiny.

Argyris (1982) developed what he called the Ladder of Inference, and this is a very helpful way of explaining how assumptions are made. The Ladder has seven steps which can be applied to research in these ways:

- **Step 1 – Observation.** At the foot of the Ladder, we observe an event as it happens. Researchers usually say that they have an open mind in relation to what they might find and are sincere about this.

- **Step 2 – Selection.** However, not only because they have already formed some opinions about their chosen area, but also because of the millions of messages their

brains receive every day, they might well select the data they need or want at any given time.

- **Step 3 – Meaning.** They then add meaning to that data from their current situation and past experiences. This meaning is drawn from their personal and cultural settings.

- **Step 4 – Assumptions.** This leads them to make assumptions about the data.

- **Step 5 – Conclusions.** From there they draw conclusions about what the data is saying.

- **Step 6 – Beliefs.** These conclusions then become part of the researcher's beliefs about the world and how it operates.

- **Step 7 – Action.** The researcher then takes action based on their beliefs.

Following on from this, the researcher can take what Argyris calls one of two recursive loops. The first is from Step 6 (Beliefs) to Step 2 (Selection). By doing this, their beliefs lead them to make choices about the data they select in the future. This means that they will often tend to select the data that confirms what they believe and ignore the data that does not. The second loop is from Step 7 (Action) at the top of the Ladder to Step 1 (Observation) at the bottom. This means they take action to seek more observable data. But the data gathered is based on their beliefs, which encourage them to see what they have seen before. This leads to bias in favour of what they have seen already. By following either of these recursive loops, their assumptions are confirmed and their beliefs are reinforced.

Try this

Think about your own position in relation to your research and any assumptions you might be making. How might you be able to guard against these?

Maintaining confidentiality and keeping your data secure

The importance of confidentiality has already been highlighted in Theme 6.2, and we explore this further here. Anyone who agrees to take part in a research study is likely to disclose things about themselves (for example, their thoughts, opinions, actions, behaviours) and does so in an atmosphere of trust. As a result, you need to make sure that you apply these principles:

- That no participant can be identified. This particularly comes to the fore in relation to qualitative research where individual participants are interviewed. In all circumstances make sure that each participant is anonymised by using a pseudonym; be sure to change their name sufficiently so that anyone who knows them will not be able to identify them. It is also good practice to give them a pseudonym that represents their cultural and/or ethnic heritage.

- Make locations anonymous too. For example, if you were carrying out quantitative or qualitative research in a school, change the name of the school. For the particular school to remain unidentifiable you might also need to

change any reference to the geographical area too by broadening it. In the case of a rural school, you might need to replace the name of the village with the name of the county, and in the case of a city school, you might need to replace the name of the district with the name of the city, or even the region.

- Be sure to use the data gathered only for the purpose of your study and keep it securely. This means keeping any paer copies (for example, of questionnaires) private and out of the sight of other people. Any recordings (for example, of research interviews) should be listened to only by you. All data should be password-protected whenever possible and destroyed when the study is complete.

Keeping data secure and confidential is an important part of the research process, but there are times when confidentiality cannot be guaranteed. For example, if a participant disclosed some kind of illegal activity, you would need to report it, otherwise as a researcher you would be complicit in it and could subsequently face prosecution for assisting in the crime by failing to tell someone.

Safeguarding issues can also emerge, so if a participant shared something that showed that they were at risk of harm, you would want to know that they had the relevant support available. How to do this will be discussed further in the next section.

Try this

Think about the steps you will need to take to protect the data you are gathering.

Theme 6.5 — Gaining informed consent

Gaining the informed consent of participants is another important part of the research process and is essential in order to carry out a study ethically. People who take part in a study need to know what it involves, what will be expected of them and what will happen with the data they share. Trust and honesty are key factors in making sure that you establish and maintain an effective relationship with your research participants.

Consent can be given verbally, but asking participants for written consent is often recommended because it is clearer and more precise. It can be easy to agree to something verbally only to regret it later. Written consent should offer participants the detail they need to decide whether or not they wish to take part in the study. In addition, having something in writing can be read later if clarification is needed. Written consent can be requested in an email or letter and can also be incorporated into a questionnaire.

Formulating a request for consent takes time and should include:

- **the purpose of the research** – for a dissertation or independent study;

- **what the research will involve** – a brief statement of the main features of the research from the point of view of a participant, such as a questionnaire or interview, the conditions under which it will be carried out (for example, recorded) and the time involved;

- **the right to withdraw** at any point without having to give an explanation;

- **the care given to information shared** – that it will be treated in confidence and that no participant will be named in any written work arising from the study;

- **the use of the material** – that all material (verbal and written) will be used solely for the purpose of the study and will be destroyed when it has been completed;

- **space for the participant to sign.**

Some universities provide students with a consent form that is ready to use; others have templates that you can use to devise your own. Do check with your tutor or supervisor, as either of these could save you some valuable time.

Notes

In some areas of research, it is possible that safeguarding issues might arise. In certain areas, taking part in research can cause distress or anxiety to participants. If this is a possibility, it is good practice to highlight sources of support that participants can access, and this can be done on the consent form. That way, participants will know who to go to if they are affected adversely by taking part in the study.

Case Study

Researching a sensitive topic

Joanne is studying for a degree in sociology and is interested in issues concerning suicide among young men. In particular, she wants to know what makes them more reluctant to seek help and support than their female counterparts, something that is supported through an experience she had with a close friend. Initially she wanted to explore this area by handing out questionnaires to some of her fellow male students, but during a discussion about this with her supervisor it soon became clear that this would not be possible because of important ethical issues, such as the harm it could potentially cause to participants. In the light of this she decided to undertake desk research where she examined some secondary data.

More food for thought

In carrying out research it is very easy to see what we expect to see, or even what we would like to see. Rather than keeping true to the well-known phrase 'I'll believe it when I see it' (or, 'I'll believe it when I have examined the evidence for it'), we can easily slip into 'I believe it, so I see it'. This means that we simply see what we expect to see and discount anything that does not conform to our existing ideas. Doing this in the context of research is problematic not only in relation to subjectivity and bias; it also means that our results are predictable, leaving the reader thinking, 'Well, they were always going to say that, weren't they?'

So now think about how you can avoid this. Here are two possibilities:

- Question everything often by asking yourself 'Is that always the case?'

- Be open and actively seek out some contrary data that will disconfirm your assumptions.

Alex's journal 6

Supervision was so helpful today! Thank goodness I decided to be brave and share my methodology stuff — turns out I had understood more than I thought. I'd love to get people's thoughts on single-use plastic but can see now that I know what I'd like people to say ('it's terrible, we should ban it completely!'), so I don't think that's a good idea! So I am now thinking about various ideas, like:

- doing an observation in the coffee shop for half an hour at lunchtime to see how many items are bought that are contained in single-use plastic. Positivist, quantitative but really not sure what this will tell me that I don't know already — that it's loads and far too much for my liking;

- talking to people buying the stuff about what they feel. Interpretivist, qualitative, and may well be too subjective;

- talking to coffee shop managers and someone in the university's sustainability team about what they're doing to reduce its use. Interpretivist and qualitative again but could be quite interesting.

Need to think about this more. Supervisor says it must all be doable, and I know they're right.

Theme 7

Support and feedback

This section will:

- give you a picture of how supervision works;

- enable you to build a positive relationship with your supervisor;

- help you to think about how to use the feedback you get;

- introduce you to the concept of critical friendship;

- help you to think about what to do if you get into difficulties.

Theme 7.1

The supervisory relationship

As part of the research process you will be allocated a supervisor; this person will usually work with you from the point at which your proposal is accepted by the ethics committee through to the completion of your study. Your supervisor might be someone you know already (for example, a tutor who has taught one of your previous modules) or it could be someone new. Understanding the role of the supervisor is key when thinking about how you can work together effectively. There are things that a good supervisor will and will not do; there are some examples in Table 5, and you might be able to think of more.

You might work with your supervisor on an individual level or in a small group; this is for your supervisor to stipulate and to organise. Group supervision can be very helpful as it gives you the opportunity to learn from your fellow students as well as from the tutor. It saves time too as many students have similar concerns. It is good to remember that most supervisors are very busy, so their time will be limited. It will be important to work with them effectively in order to get as much as you can from the small amount of time they can offer you. We examine this in some detail in the next theme.

Notes

Table 5: Supervisory relationships

A good supervisor will	A good supervisor will not
Treat all students with respect	Treat any student disrespectfully
Guide you through the process of your research	Tell you what to do
Offer you support and encouragement	Nag you or remind you of what you need to do when this is clear in relevant and accessible documentation
Offer sessions to individuals and/or groups at a scheduled time and in a designated place	See you only when and where it suits you
Be happy to hear about the progress you are making	Be happy to hear that you have done little work on your study
Want to help you to study independently	Allow you to become dependent on them
Assume everything is okay if they haven't heard from you	Contact you if you don't reply to their messages
Point you in the right direction for support they are not able to give	Answer every small query you might have

Building a good relationship with your supervisor

The relationship you have with your supervisor will be one of the most important relationships you have during your programme of study, so it is worth thinking about how to approach this. Like any working relationship it will be good to put some time and effort into building it, and here are some things you can do that can make a real difference:

- **Make initial contact** – when you know who your supervisor is going to be, contact them straightaway. They will probably have received a list of the students they will be supervising and a nice, informal introductory message from you will help to cement you in their minds as one of their new supervisees. It shows you are interested and enthusiastic, which is always a good thing; first impressions are important. Sending an initial email is likely to be a good method of communication as they can then reply when they are available. Tell them a bit about your research, how your ideas (including your research questions) have been developing and that you have been doing some initial reading. That way they can see that you are looking ahead and will welcome their feedback

as your work progresses. In addition, don't be afraid to send them the latest copy of your research proposal; this will save them time looking for it.

- **Be organised** – we have already said a lot about the importance of planning and taking an organised approach, and this applies to supervision too. Once you have heard from your supervisor, block out the time needed on your schedule for any meetings. If the supervisor holds an initial meeting (individual or group) you should not miss this; the supervisor will use this to explain how they want to work with you. Be sure to attend the meeting and then work in the way that they prefer whenever possible. This might include regular email contact, attending group or individual sessions and taking part in recommended sessions provided by central services (for example, literature review, referencing, academic language). Supervisors will only suggest things that they know will be helpful to you.

- **Keep in regular contact** – as well as attending supervision sessions, you will probably have some email contact with your supervisor. There are some things to be mindful of in order to continue to build your positive working relationship, and much of this is about striking the right balance; so, not too much contact and not too little, and not when you can find the advice easily elsewhere (such as on your VLE, in your handbook or by asking a fellow student or an administrator).

- **Take a conscientious approach** – all supervisors enjoy working with students who take their research seriously, work hard and want to do well.

- **Be open-minded** – supervisors are there to guide, support and give feedback, and being open to this is a vital part of the supervisory process.

Try this

Think about how you can be a good supervisee. Are there any particular steps you need to take to ensure a positive working relationship with your supervisor?

Theme 7.3 Making the most of feedback

Good feedback is vital for your academic development, so it is important to understand what it is and how to use it effectively. During your research study you will receive feedback from your supervisor and possibly from your fellow students too, especially if some of your supervision is done in a group. However, not all feedback is good and having an understanding of this will give you indicators of when you might need to ask for more.

Good feedback is:

- respectful of your work;

- helpful and supportive;

- honest and given with integrity – good supervisors always want their students to achieve their potential;

- specific and focused on things that you need to change or work on to develop further;

- timely – not too soon and not too late;

- limited in amount – there is only so much feedback that a person can cope with at any one time;

- clear and clarified if necessary, to avoid any misunderstandings;

- focused on positives with some points for further development to enable you to make progress;

- motivating – helping you to achieve your end goal.

Good feedback is not:

- disrespectful of your work;

- accusatory;

- unhelpful;

- undermining;

- judgemental;

- too much to take in at once;

- vague and woolly;

- only focused on negatives.

Feedback can help you to see things that you wouldn't otherwise see; this is sometimes referred to as a 'blind area' (Luft, 1984). Understanding what good feedback is helps you to process it when you receive it. This in turn helps you to act on it in order to move your work forward.

Good supervisory relationships are built on mutual respect, but this does not necessarily mean that feedback is always easy to receive or that you will always agree with what your supervisor says. A good supervisor will always want to hear your arguments for your approach, and ultimately this will help you when it comes to writing up your work for submission.

Try this

Think about the areas of your work where you might need feedback at this point. What might you need in the future and where might you get this from (for example, your supervisor, fellow students, central services)?

The role of a critical friend

While undertaking your research you may well find it helpful to work with a critical friend. There are things in life that a good friend should and will tell us (for example, when we have broccoli in our teeth!). A friend will be honest while being sensitive to how we feel. A critical friend is another person who can support you in your research and give you feedback on relevant aspects of it.

So, what makes a good critical friend? They should be:

- someone who you know and can trust – friends do not steal from one another, and this applies to ideas and academic work as well here;

- a good listener;

- someone who asks questions sensitively that challenge your thinking and your approach;

- someone who always acts with integrity and has your interests at heart;

- someone who is positive, constructive and encouraging;

- someone who is not afraid to discuss any apparent weaknesses in your research, as well as its strengths.

The core qualities of a strong critical friendship are similar to those of supervision, and include:

- mutual respect;

- trust on both sides;

- openness and honesty;

- a good mutual understanding.

A vital part of being an effective critical friend is to take a sensitive and questioning approach. A good critical friend is not negative or destructive but helps their friend to examine their approach to their research with a critical eye. Often a good place to start is to ask the important 'what' question, for example, 'What made you take that particular approach?' That way you ask your friend to defend their position, which means they have to think things through in a more robust way. This will help them when they write their research report or dissertation later on.

104

You may feel you already have someone who fulfils the role of a critical friend, but if not you will want to choose them carefully. It is worth remembering that it may not be your best friend and should be someone whom you can rely on to ask you challenging questions. In the long run, this will be more helpful than someone who will just say that they think everything is good as it is at the moment.

Try this

Think about someone you could work with as a critical friend. If you already have a critical friend, how can you best work with them so that you can both get the most from it?

What to do if you experience difficulties

Carrying out a research study is often a lengthy process completed over a semester or even a whole academic year. Because of this, it rarely goes completely smoothly and there will often be some challenges along the way. In this section we explore what to do if you find yourself experiencing difficulties.

The first thing to remember is that it is never good to bury your head in the sand and hope that the difficulties will simply go away. It is always best to speak to your supervisor at the earliest opportunity because there will often be support available from a number of different sources. Some of these will be familiar to you already and you may even have used some of them before. Here are three general pointers to help you:

- If you are carrying out empirical research and things are not going to plan (for example, contacts have let you down or participants have withdrawn) speak to your supervisor about making alternative plans. This could mean using other contacts, or, if an alternative solution cannot be found, you might discuss doing some secondary research or a literature review instead.

- If you are experiencing personal difficulties, speak to your personal tutor (often called your personal academic tutor). They are usually your first point of contact when personal issues arise and can often make contact with your course or programme director (or will ask you to contact them) as they have the authority to grant such things as an extension to your submission deadline on the grounds of extenuating circumstances. In some situations, they might suggest you contact the university's student counselling service or other appropriate services such as finance.

- If you are experiencing academic difficulties, do be sure to access any services that are provided centrally (for example, through the library). These might include workshops on topics like referencing and writing a literature review; some libraries also offer individual support, including literature search and proofreading. It is a good idea to find out what is on offer in advance just in case you need it.

Notes

When challenges come your way, it is often easy to think that you are the only one experiencing difficulties, but this is rarely the case. Speaking to your fellow students and other friends can also be very helpful and should mean that you will then feel less isolated. Be sure to get the support you need when you need it; in general, this is not a sign of weakness, and knowing when to ask for help is a strength and often the first step towards overcoming whatever is holding you back.

More food for thought

Now spend some time thinking about how best to work with your supervisor; remember it should be kept on a professional level at all times. You will probably have contact with your supervisor by email reasonably regularly, and here are some things to avoid:

- language that is more suited to text messages;

- writing in incomplete sentences;

- language that is too familiar;

- using emoticons;

- messages where you just 'let off steam' about something without looking at how to solve a problem or issue.

How does your supervisor seem to prefer to work?

Space for your thoughts

Alex's journal 7

Long chat today with people in my supervision group. Really need to decide what I'm doing or I'm going to get badly behind with everything. Seems like some people are already well ahead, but I think it's always like that. People in the group helped me to see that the whole thing must be practical otherwise it just won't get done.

Walking back to the library and thinking everything through again. Going to ask a couple of coffee shop managers if I can talk to them and email someone in the university's sustainability team to see if I can talk to them about what the uni is doing about reducing the amount of single-use plastic.

Feels really good to have made a decision — now time to get on!

Top Tip

Be open-minded

Carrying out a research study successfully requires a sharp focus, and it is easy to become immersed in it. As we have seen, feedback will be an important part of the learning process, and having an open mind will be to your advantage. Here are some points to help you to stay receptive to new ideas:

- In the social sciences there are usually no single correct answers (even in quantitative research), so we need to be open to multiple explanations of phenomena. If you find yourself thinking you have found 'the answer', ask yourself what the opposing arguments are and explore relevant literature that supports the alternative views. These can then be added to your literature review to make it even stronger.

- Many supervisors have views on how they like things to be done. While you may not always agree with them, they have lots of experience in this area, and it is always worth considering their suggestions. If you still disagree with them, be sure to be able to give clear and strong reasons for not taking their advice. At undergraduate level, your supervisor often has the responsibility for marking your dissertation too, although it will usually be marked by another tutor or supervisor as well. In such cases it is even more important to be able to state clearly and with conviction why you have not taken their advice and to use supporting evidence.

- Taking a questioning approach to your own work is often helpful. Questions like 'Is that always the case?' and 'Who takes the opposite viewpoint?' will help you to keep an open mind. In addition, asking the question 'Says who?' will help you to support your arguments with reference to relevant literature.

Notes

It is not always easy to receive feedback, especially if we don't agree with it. However, taking feedback on board will usually help our overall development and might lead to higher marks; something that everyone ultimately wants.

Theme 8 Research management

This section will:

- help you to understand how to manage your research project;
- help you to understand what to do when things don't go according to plan;
- enable you to think about how to cope with the unexpected;
- help you to start thinking about data analysis;
- enable you to think about what to do with large amounts of data.

Theme 8.1

Managing your research project

In Theme 3.1 we discussed devising a plan to help you to organise your study. Research studies are usually carried out fairly independently, so you need to be prepared to manage it yourself rather than expecting someone else to do it for you. This is excellent preparation for future work where you might be expected to show initiative and manage your workload without close supervision. Of course, at university there is always support at hand, but you need to be ready to ask for it.

So, how can you manage your research effectively and to your advantage? Having devised an initial plan by working back from your submission date (see Theme 3.1) you will probably have to review it as time goes on, so you continue to make progress. Drucker once famously said, 'Plans are just good intentions unless they immediately degenerate into hard work', and his management by objectives model (Drucker, 1954) could be a useful tool. Written as a model for business, it has been adapted here for the context of your research study. It involves these five steps:

- review your goals;

- look back at your research tasks;

- monitor your own progress;

- evaluate your performance so far;

- reward yourself.

As in many areas of life, different approaches work for different people, and the most important thing is to find what works for you. Many people (including myself) like to work on something step by step from start to finish; it gives a clear structure and a sense of purpose. However, when it comes to a research study this often won't work well and can even be a hindrance. For example, if you try and write a full introduction as a starting point, it can often be difficult. The first and last sentences or paragraphs in any piece of written work are often the most difficult things to write, and it is easy to get stuck. Leaving them until later often works better.

The nature of research projects means that we often need to work on more than one thing in any given period. Looking at the Research Triangle, on page 158, is helpful at this point, and the bullet points on pages 34–35 show how you might well need to continue to refine your research questions, engage with reading relevant literature and analyse the data you have collected in an ongoing way as the project proceeds. An introduction will probably include your research questions (those 'tent poles' that support the whole piece), so writing this very early in the process, only to have to go back and amend it several times, can be very frustrating.

Try this

Think about how you can take your research forward from this point. Allen's (2015) four-criteria model could be useful.

- **Context** – what can I do here?

- **Time available** – what time do I have now?

- **Energy available** – how much energy do I have at the moment?

- **Priority** – what are the most important tasks that need to be done?

Write some notes for each of these questions.

What to do when things don't go according to plan

Having a detailed plan is always a positive thing, but most research projects do not always go completely to plan. Thinking of your plan as a working document is a good idea, and you should amend it as and when you need to do so. This will ensure that it remains useful as your study progresses. Here are some examples of things that can commonly happen during a research project that might not be in your plan, with some tips on how to address them:

- **Things take longer than anticipated** – as part of your planning process you will have estimated the amount of time aspects of the project should take; this is not an exact science and can leave you thinking 'How long is a piece of string?' Most commonly, people find things take longer (sometimes significantly longer) than they think. At such times you will need to adjust your plan but be sure to do so in relation to your whole plan by looking ahead. If you amend only certain parts of it, you could find yourself running out of time later on as the submission date begins to approach.

- **Things happen too quickly** – while on the surface this might seem like a good problem to have, it can also cause

difficulties. For example, participants might want or need to take part sooner than you expected. This is fine if you have everything you need well prepared in advance, but if you are still working on your research methods (for example, devising a questionnaire or an interview schedule) you will probably need to ask participants to wait until you are ready. You could ask them to take part in a pilot study at that point to help you develop your methods. In many situations, gathering data before you are ready really isn't a good option as you won't have time, or be able, to go back later and do it all again if you feel you need to do so.

- **Personal things get in the way** – in my experience this is the most common reason for things not going to plan. Life always has the potential to throw something at us when we least expect it; significant illness and bereavement are two examples. At times like this you need to make your supervisor aware of your situation as soon as possible. Also, be sure to access all the support you can from other sources (see Theme 7.5), including applying for a later submission date because of extenuating circumstances when appropriate.

Notes

While it can be frustrating when things don't go according to plan, being flexible in your approach will help you to stay resilient in the face of challenges. Keeping the end goal in mind and having the determination to finish should pay off in the end.

Coping with the unexpected

We can also experience difficulties when things come up that we don't expect. This can happen in several different ways during a research project, and it is easy to let these get in the way of the progress we want and often need to make. Sometimes it might feel like we are 'stalling', as it can take time to work out a way forward. Here are some examples of unexpected things that can happen and some possible ways of dealing with them:

- **Participants withdraw** – sometimes even the keenest participant can decide that they can no longer take part in a study, or no longer wish to do so. This is their prerogative, and while it is always disappointing it is sadly not rare. If you have thought ahead, you might already have someone else in reserve, but this won't always be possible. In any case, it will be important to act quickly to find a replacement.

- **Relevant permission is withheld** – in the case of research carried out in a particular setting (for example, a school) permission to carry out the research there might be denied. This can happen even when it has been agreed previously, for example if there is a change in staffing. Finding an alternative quickly will again be important, although it might also be possible for the research to be carried out on other premises instead (for example, in the university), depending on the particular research study.

- **Things disappear from the internet** – this might sound strange, but sources can be withdrawn from the internet without prior warning. For example, a film or documentary that you plan to examine as part of your study suddenly disappears without trace. You might be able to find it using the internet archive Wayback Machine (2014), or it might mean finding an alternative source quickly that fulfils a similar function.

In circumstances like these it is easy to panic and even to freeze. But being flexible and finding alternatives will help you to continue to move forward. Here are some points to bear in mind:

- **Speak to your supervisor** – it is good to make sure they are aware of what is happening, and a good supervisor will

Notes

help you to think through some appropriate strategies for getting your study back on track. They are a good sounding board but remember they won't tell you what to do.

- Use your contacts and your contacts' contacts – speak to people you know (for example your fellow students) and ask them to ask people they know. This way you broaden out your field of possibilities.

- Think about what you can still do – it might be that you will still be able to gather some data even if some participants withdraw or some of your sources disappear from the internet. It's always good to see what you can salvage, even if it is only a small part.

It is fair to say that most desk research or a literature review is more predictable than most empirical research. If your empirical research looks as if it might collapse, desk research or a literature review can offer a reliable alternative and can alleviate a lot of stress along the way.

Getting ready to analyse your data

One significant element of managing your research project will be thinking about how you will analyse your data. This can be done in a number of ways depending on whether your study uses a quantitative or qualitative method, and your sessions on research methods should help you in this regard. When thinking about this particular area, the first step is to go back to your research questions. As your study progresses it is likely that you will revisit these to refine and amend them. This process continues right through data analysis, as what your data reveals becomes clearer.

Thinking about how to code your data is an important precursor to carrying out your analysis, and it will be very useful to do some preparation for it in good time (Bergin, 2018). Coding means applying labels to data (both quantitative and qualitative) that describe its content and enables the process of recognising and devising themes; these facilitate data analysis. On a practical level, coding can be done in several different ways (for example, using highlighters, sticky notes, labels, different-coloured pens or text).

Before you start coding, here are some things to consider:

- **Revisit relevant research methods materials** – as part of your research methods module or sessions you will have had input on data analysis. However, at that particular point you are inevitably examining data analysis in the abstract so you may well need to go back to your notes on the relevant session to be able to apply it in practice effectively.

- **Re-read the sections on data analysis in your 'go-to' book on research methods** – this is likely to explain the different ways you could analyse your data in a way that you can understand easily.

- **Attend a refresher workshop on data analysis** – many universities offer these because they understand that as time goes by, things can be forgotten or need to be revisited.

- **Request a discussion with your supervisor** – sometimes this can help if you are particularly unsure about which approach to take.

- **Don't be afraid to try one or two different approaches** – it is not always possible to decide beforehand how you will analyse your data, so briefly trying one or two different approaches can help.

Good data analysis is strong and can stand up to some scrutiny, so it is well worth thinking your approach through carefully. Poor data analysis can lead to weak conclusions which can in turn affect how your study is perceived and, of course, the mark you ultimately achieve.

Try this

Think about the different approaches you could take when analysing your data.

Theme 8.5 — Dealing with large amounts of data

Many people who carry out empirical research find that they collect a lot of data, whether this is via questionnaires, interviews or other methods. Hopefully you will be carrying out research in an area that you are interested in, so it is likely that you will find the data you are collecting interesting as well. A large amount of data needs to be managed well, otherwise it is all too easy to feel swamped by it. You will have to make decisions about which data to select. This can be difficult, particularly when you have collected data that is relevant to your topic and have invested time in its collection.

As part of your analysis it is likely that you will need to select which data to include; often it is not possible to include everything. So where do you start? Here are some ideas to help you, and they act as another reminder of the Research Triangle (see Figure 10 on page 158):

- **Go back to your research questions again** – these should guide you to the data that is most useful and relevant to your study.

- **Go back to your literature review** – this should also highlight aspects that you could focus on.

- **Look for the data that you find the most striking** – this can be very subjective, but it is always worth looking for things that surprise you. These could be things that are different from what you expected and even things that are not supported by literature. Here it might be that there is something new that could help you gain high marks for aspects of originality. It could also help you to point to further research that could be done in this area as part of your conclusions.

There are two other things that can occur as part of the data analysis process. The first is that you find you have collected data that does not relate closely to your research questions, so much so that it makes your study very different from the one that gained ethical approval. It is usually not advisable or even possible to go right back to the beginning again; there simply is not enough time. The second is that you find that you have no data on a particular research question; in this case do talk to your supervisor. It might be wise to delete this particular question and focus on the rest. A discussion of this process can then be added to the section where you critically evaluate your study.

Selecting which data to include often involves making tough decisions. Of course, this can also happen in the process of doing secondary research or a literature review. Having invested a lot of time and effort in your study, it can be difficult to let go of data, but most researchers have to do this to produce a study that is clear and concise and has a sharp focus.

Try this

Think about the choices you might be facing in relation to the data you have collected either from primary or secondary sources, or from a literature review.

More food for thought

There are two useful tools that can help you to manage your research:

- **a Gantt chart** – shows week by week what you need to focus on and can be a helpful visual reminder (see Figure 8);

- **a mind map** – gives you a visual representation (see Figure 9).

Now think about which of these might help you at the moment.

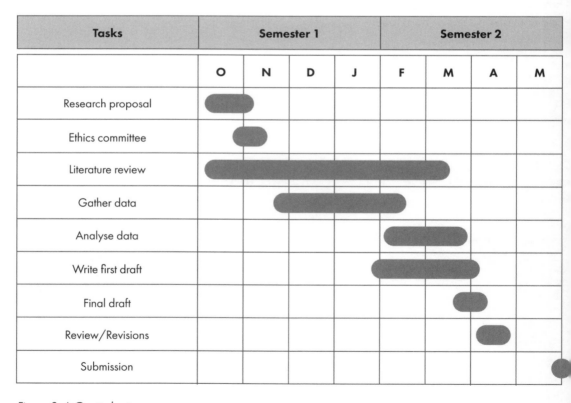

Tasks	Semester 1				Semester 2			
	O	N	D	J	F	M	A	M
Research proposal	▬							
Ethics committee		▬						
Literature review	▬	▬	▬	▬	▬			
Gather data			▬	▬	▬			
Analyse data						▬		
Write first draft					▬	▬		
Final draft							▬	
Review/Revisions							▬	
Submission								▬

Figure 8: A Gantt chart

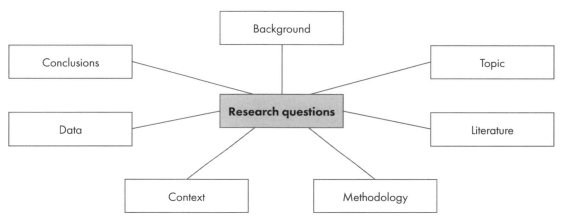

Figure 9: A mind map

Alex's journal 8

Spoke to two coffee shop managers today and they have agreed to be interviewed about reducing single-use plastic — result! Now need to get on and devise my interview questions. Shouldn't be too difficult now I know what I'm doing — famous last words! Will send them to my supervisor when I've written them, to be on the safe side.

Hopefully this will give me some interesting data. Still haven't heard back from the sustainability office, so I'm going to pop in tomorrow and see if I can ask someone — nothing ventured, nothing gained!

'Big rocks first'

Managing any large project is a big task in itself, and Covey (2004) gives us another reminder of the importance of planning by using a very helpful visual metaphor. He describes time as an empty vessel (think of a large transparent tank) that we fill up with a variety of things.

In relation to a research project these would be as follows:

- **big rocks** – important tasks that help us to achieve our goals (for example, reading relevant literature, devising a questionnaire, constructing interview questions, writing up the research report or dissertation);

- **pebbles** – smaller tasks that get in the way and are not necessarily important (for example reading literature that we find interesting but that doesn't relate to our study, browsing online for resources that we don't really need);

- **sand** – things that we don't really need to do (for example, time spent on social media and email);

- **water** – things that we do that we can't even remember, which seem to make time disappear (for example, browsing on the internet.

The size of the tank remains the same; we all have the same amount of time each day. But how much we can put into the tank will vary depending on what we put in first. Without even thinking about it, many of us fill up much of our tank (or even all of it) with sand and water. We then wonder why we don't have room for the pebbles and, in particular, the rocks. Covey's advice is simple; put the rocks in first (focus on the important things) and there will still be room for other things too, as they fill up the spaces between the rocks. Trying to put your rocks in later when your tank is already full of pebbles, sand and water simply won't work.

Space for your thoughts

Theme 9 Motivation

This section will:

- help you to examine your motivation for your research;

- help you to understand more about the role of emotions in your research;

- help you to be ready for peaks and troughs;

- discuss strategies for when you feel like giving up;

- help you to understand more about why it all feels so important.

What motivates you in your research?

Understanding what motivates you can be an important factor in helping you to keep going and finish a research project. Motivation is an abstract concept which is difficult to define, but it usually includes the factors and processes that prompt us to do things in certain ways. It also includes why we fail to complete things.

There are many theories that seek to explain what motivation is and they can be classified into two main groups: content and process theories. In addition, theories of motivation often identify factors that motivate people; some of these are external (extrinsic) and some are internal (intrinsic). Here are two examples of each:

Content – theories that describe what motivation is:

- Maslow's (1954) hierarchy of need – probably one of the best-known theories of motivation. Usually depicted as a pyramid, it asserts that we are motivated to satisfy our basic biological and physiological needs (for example, food and water) at the base of the pyramid before we can satisfy other higher-order needs such as self-actualisation (sometimes described as fulfilling our potential).

- McGregor's (1970) X and Y theory – developed from the work of Maslow. This argues that there are two types of people in relation to motivation. Type X are motivated by their biological and safety needs at the bottom of Maslow's hierarchy, or by extrinsic factors. Type Y are motivated by the top three levels (love, esteem and self-actualisation) – by extrinsic factors (such as rewards) and intrinsic ones too (for example, a sense of achievement).

Process – theories that describe how people are motivated:

- Vroom's (1964) expectancy theory – people make choices based on the reward they expect to receive. People value different outcomes and work in proportion to how much they feel they will achieve. So, people put in a lot of effort if they feel their chances of success are high, and vice versa.

- Adams's (1965) equity theory – focuses on fairness. People are motivated when they feel they are receiving equal treatment. The converse is also true, so they feel de-motivated if they sense they are being treated unfairly compared to others in a similar position.

In addition, many writers on the subject of motivation speak of the importance of setting goals as part of the process (see Theme 3.3). In more recent research, Pink (2009) proposes that motivation is made up of three key elements:

- **autonomy** – having some control over your own work;

- **mastery** – working on something in detail to get better at it;

- **purpose** – connecting with a larger vision or goal.

All of these seem to have a clear role in relation to the motivation to complete a research project.

In relation to your research, understanding more about what motivates you should help you to continue to make progress. At appropriate points in the process it is well worth asking yourself why you might not be making as much progress as you would like and identifying any barriers to motivation will be important. You can then take appropriate action to overcome them.

Try this

Think about what motivates you in your research. Which theory of motivation best describes how you are motivated, and why? What barriers are you facing and how might you overcome them?

The role of emotions in research

Anything that involves a commitment of time will probably mean that we make an emotional investment in it, and a research study is no exception to this. This means that we can develop an attachment (sometimes a strong attachment) to it and it can prompt some strong feelings. This can bring difficulties with it, and understanding more about how this plays out in practice can be useful in helping us to continue to succeed.

As human beings we all have emotional responses to things, but we often fail to understand what triggers these and why they can be so powerful. Sometimes the strength of our feelings can take us by surprise and Riches' (2012) work on the Almond Effect is useful in explaining why this happens. Neuroscience shows that our brains are designed to respond to threatening situations with a 'fight or flight' response. These responses are automatic and are the result of the hardwiring of our neural pathways. They were learned through the process of evolution and have acted as a key survival mechanism for the human race. In the brain we each have two almond-shaped sets of neurons called amygdalae (from the Greek word for almond); these play a vital role in stimulating and regulating our emotional responses, particularly in relation to fear, prompting a 'fight

or flight' response. Riches explains that our instinctive emotional responses always happen first, followed by our rational ones.

There are many things in research that can trigger an emotional response in us. For example, feedback (see Theme 7.3) is not always easy to receive, especially if we don't agree with it, if we find it harsh in some way or if we are simply having a bad day. This can make us feel angry or defensive. We can become disappointed, even despondent, when participants withdraw, and can take this too personally. Riches speaks of a 'Mindfield', where the Almond Effect prompts us to respond quickly and emotionally. In these circumstances, she advises us to step back and take time to think things through. This way we will reach a more rational response, which will often enable us to continue and complete things more effectively.

Peters (2012: 4) introduces us to the concept of the Chimp (the area of the brain called the limbic) which he describes as 'the emotional machine'. This emotional machine is paradoxical because it can be our best friend or our worst enemy. He says we need to learn to live with it, discipline it, harness its strengths and not let it rule our lives.

Notes

Think about times when you have had an emotional response to your study. What happened and how did you deal with it?

Dealing with peaks and troughs

Anything that takes a period of time to complete is bound to have its peaks and troughs. In the beginning most students start a research study because of a particular interest they have in a topic. Often it will be prompted by a previous module where they would have liked to explore something in more depth but didn't have the time. These are good reasons for choosing an area to research. However, as time progresses some ups and downs are inevitable, and at times it can feel as if you have grown to have a 'love-hate' relationship with the project. At this point it is good to think about how to make the most of the peaks and how to survive the troughs.

Making the most of the peaks sounds like the easy part, and in many ways it is, or at least it should be. At these times it is good to keep going and to take full advantage of the energy and enthusiasm you have without spending too much time thinking about it. This is because it is all too easy to sit back, relax and lose focus. Before you know it, a sense of 'This is a lot easier than I thought' can make you take your foot off the metaphorical accelerator, slow down, and you quickly fall behind. I rarely hear a student say they are finding it difficult being so far ahead of where they thought they would be!

Working through the troughs is often more difficult. At times like this it is essential to keep going, so your study does not come to a complete halt. Here are some ideas to help you:

- **Take a short break** – the word to emphasise here is 'short'. Sometimes things can be difficult simply because we are tired, so having a relaxing break and a good night's sleep can really help. We will then find we have more energy and make progress more quickly; this encourages us, and we make even more progress as a result. But remember, taking a long break can have a negative effect as it can be very difficult to get going again.

- **Speak to someone** – see the sources of support discussed in Theme 7 and draw on them if and when you feel you need to do so.

- **Do the next bit of planning** – this is time invested not wasted. It helps you to take a step back, look at your overall progress and start to move forward again.

- **Break the work down into smaller parts** – in Theme 3.1 we discussed the salami method. When things become difficult, everything can seem much bigger, and breaking things down into smaller parts can help us to feel that they are more manageable. Instead of having a goal of writing your methodology section, think about writing 500 words of it instead. You might find that the whole thing feels much more achievable.

- **Keep a list of things you have done** – we know about the value of 'to-do lists' but having a 'done list' can be a very good motivator too.

- **Use your passion** – remember why you chose your study in the first place.

- **Don't be too hard on yourself** – remember how far you have come.

- **Stop comparing yourself with other people** – there will always be people who seem to be further ahead than you are. Focus on yourself and what you want to achieve next.

Peaks and troughs in research are inevitable, so it is good to enjoy the peaks and persevere through the troughs. It will definitely be worth it.

What to do when you feel like giving up

There are times in many research studies when people feel it is all too difficult and they want to give up. Tempting as this might feel at that particular point in time, the cost of actually doing so is usually a price that is too great to pay, and this thought keeps us going. At such times we might well have experienced some setbacks that have put obstacles in our way; some of these might be practical and others personal.

At times like this, processing our feelings is particularly helpful. Boud, Keogh and Walker (1985) put forward a very useful model where they encourage us to pay attention to our feelings so that we can address them. Their model consists of three stages:

- **Returning to the experience** – this involves looking back on what has been happening and could include discussing it with others.

- **Attending to feelings** – this means paying attention to our feelings and involves two key aspects: building on the positive ones and removing those that are negative or obstructive.

- **Re-evaluating the experience** – this is the most important stage; the new knowledge we have is added to what we know already, and we begin to move forward as we think about things differently.

They argue that if we don't process our feelings and take appropriate action as a result, it is likely that the negative or obstructive ones, in particular, will remain and could thereby become a significant barrier to our development. So, thoughts like, 'I didn't think I could do this and now I know I can't' can take over.

Processing feelings involves externalising them and this can be done in a number of ways. Writing in a journal like this can help; some people experience a sense of release as they put their thoughts on to paper, getting them out of their head and leaving them there. Others prefer to talk to a trusted friend or relative. If you find yourself in the position where you are seriously thinking of giving up, do speak to your supervisor or programme director, as there will often be a way forward even if you can't see it at the moment.

Notes

Try this

Think about any obstructive feelings you might be having in relation to your research. How might you be able to process them so that they don't become a barrier to your development?

Why does it all feel so important?

Many students I work with speak of how important their research study is, and here are some of the reasons why:

- **The number of marks involved** – a dissertation or research project often attracts a larger number of credits than a taught module, sometimes two or even three times as many. So, it rightly feels like a lot rests on it in relation to the overall grade or degree classification that could be gained.

- **'The final countdown'** – it often comes as the end point of a whole programme of study when there are lots of other things at stake, such as the job you hope to get or the postgraduate study you want to move on to.

- **They want to do themselves justice** – having worked hard, they want to do well and feel it's been worth it.

- **They don't want to let anybody down** – having been supported by staff, their fellow students, family and friends, they want others to feel proud of their achievement.

- **They don't want to let themselves down** – this can sometimes be a stronger emotion than letting others down.

- **It's a big investment** – for most people doing a degree involves investing a large amount of time and money and they simply don't want to regret it.

What they often don't recognise is that it all matters so much because they have invested a big part of themselves in it. This includes not only their time and effort, but their feelings and their relationships too. Some will even say things like, 'I've given my heart and soul to this'. However, it is good that it matters so much because then we put in the effort required and probably get a better result. Human nature is such that if it didn't matter, we wouldn't make the effort, and could then face disappointing consequences.

Space for your thoughts

More food for thought

We all need some stress in our lives in order to remain motivated, but too much stress causes distress, which can seriously hinder our progress. Now think about what you might do to avoid this or even overcome it. Here are some things that might help:

- managing your time more effectively – it's good to look back on how you have been organising yourself so you can make any possible improvements;

- being assertive and saying 'no' when you need to;

- practising some relaxation techniques – for example, doing yoga, listening to a recording designed to help you to relax;

- tapping into the support of friends and family.

Alex's journal 9

Someone in the sustainability office finally got in touch and I've arranged to interview them next week. Had to quickly get my interview questions sorted out and sent them to my supervisor. Have just heard back and they need a few changes, but generally they're ok. Phew!

Feeling really nervous about doing the interview. Seems like I'll be talking to one of the senior managers, which is a bit daunting. Going to get there early, read through my questions and try and stay calm. Really need to get a good night's sleep the night before and mustn't end up going to bed really late. Should be good!

Top Tip

Treat yourself – you deserve it!

Rewards can be a great way of keeping us motivated and they come in all shapes and sizes. It's good to think about how you can reward yourself for all your hard work on your research project and here are some ideas:

- **food glorious food!** – having a treat, for example, your favourite chocolate bar or snack;

- **time out** – taking a short break (see Theme 9.3). Planning this means you can look forward to it, which can really spur you on and keep your levels of motivation high;

- **doing something you enjoy** – going to see that film you've wanted to see for a while, going to a gig or having a meal with friends. Again, plan it so you can look forward to it;

- **doing some exercise** – helps to clear your mind. You don't have to think about anything else as you swim up and down the pool or jog round the local park. A walk can do a lot to revitalise us and can literally be a breath of fresh air. Things like this will also give you more energy;

- **spend some time resting and relaxing** – for example, with family and friends. Plan a short visit home and switch off completely.

What works for you might not necessarily work for others, so again it is good to know yourself and do those things that help you most. At times like this, planning a treat and doing it deliberately is usually much more enjoyable and beneficial than than acting on the spur of the moment. Doing something on impulse in these circumstances can make us feel that we should really be working, so we feel guilty. This often means we don't enjoy things as much and might feel that we have wasted some precious time.

Theme 10

Submission and review

This section will:

- discuss the importance of the finishing touches;

- explain the value in presenting your work to others;

- help you to think about what you would do differently;

- enable you to critically assess what you have learned about yourself;

- help you to summarise how your skills have developed.

The finishing touches

By this point you will shortly be reaching your submission point and it is good to be reminded of some of the small details that can make a difference to your final mark. They can ensure that your work is robust and 'polished', and it is well worth investing some time in them:

- **Make sure your arguments are strong** – a good piece of academic writing always has a clear central argument. In the case of a research study this is likely to be summed up in your overarching research question (see Theme 2.5) and it is well worth going back to this. Your supplementary arguments should be strong too, and remember to always present both sides.

- **Support everything** – every argument you make needs to be supported by reference to relevant literature, research or empirical evidence, otherwise it is just an assertion or an opinion.

- **Mind your language** – it must always be academic, in full sentences, grammatically correct and without jargon, abbreviations and colloquialisms. It must also be tentative, not dogmatic.

- **Your work should be presented to the highest possible standard** – be sure to edit it for errors and to proofread it carefully. Reading your work aloud can help you to see errors that you might not notice otherwise. You could also think about printing a hard copy of your work rather than reading from a computer screen as this can help with issues of presentation and layout.

- **Follow your university's presentation guidelines** – these might include the size of font to use and line spacing.

- **Make sure your references are accurate** – always use the required referencing system (Pears and Shields, 2019) and follow the formula.

- **Have an eye for detail** – by this point it's all about 'dotting the i's and crossing the t's'.

- **Know your strengths and weaknesses** – if you know you struggle in a particular area, don't be afraid to attend a refresher study skills workshop offered by central services.

Notes

Paying close attention to these final details shows that you have taken time and care in producing your work to a high standard. It will no doubt be time-consuming, but the additional marks it brings could make a real difference to your overall result.

Presenting your work to others

At some point you might be asked to present your work verbally to other people; for example, this could be to your peers or to students in the year below (van Emden and Becker, 2016). This often means presenting your work in progress, and this can be very helpful for a number of reasons:

- There is good evidence to suggest that we learn while we teach (Koh et al, 2018). You have to understand something to be able to explain it well, so presenting helps your understanding to develop, which is a very positive benefit.

- Being asked to present means you have to be ready to do it at the appointed time. This means you can't put it off and you beat procrastination.

- Preparing some visual aids is a way of summarising your work so far. Some of these could be used as diagrams or tables in your final piece of work.

- Answering questions from the audience can help you to sharpen your critique and will help you to think about where and how you can make your arguments more robust.

- It is all good preparation for the future. Many graduate recruitment processes involve delivering a presentation, and this means you won't be doing it for the first time when you go for your ideal job.

Presenting your work will always be somewhat nerve-wracking, and it is worth keeping the 4Ps in mind (Bassot, 2019):

- **Preparation** – always prepare thoroughly; few people can just stand up on the day and do it well.

- **PowerPoint** – if you put together a PowerPoint presentation, find out what is expected, for example whether you should include references or not. Make it visually attractive, professional with not too much text on each slide. Try not to read directly from it and use some notes or prompt cards instead.

- **Practice** – rehearse it several times and be sure to keep to the given time.

- **Poised** – this is about how you put yourself across, and thorough preparation will mean that you should know your material well and you can speak confidently. Rather than a verbal presentation, you might be asked to present a mind map of your research. To do this well, the same process applies, although the mind map itself will be the visual element rather than a PowerPoint presentation.

In my experience, doing a presentation, especially if it doesn't count towards your final marks, is often something that students are unenthusiastic about. However, it has many benefits; you could find that your critical thinking and your work generally really develop as a result, and it's an important landmark on the journey to your final submission.

Try this

Practice doing a presentation (for example, in front of a mirror or to a friend). How was it and what did you learn from it?

What would you do differently?

As you reach the end of the research process, it is good to spend some time looking back to review what you have done. This will be particularly useful if you are asked to write a reflective evaluation either as part of your final write-up or as a separate piece of work. Here are some areas to consider:

- If you think back to the beginning, how much have you been able to carry out what you originally set out to achieve? At this point it would be good to look back at your research proposal; you might be surprised by how much has changed and how far you have travelled on your research journey.

- Identify times when things didn't go exactly according to plan. It would be useful to reflect on what happened and what the circumstances were at those times. Consider what you might be able to learn from them. It might have been possible to avoid certain aspects, while other things might simply have been unavoidable.

- It's possible that you had to make some changes to ensure that you completed your project successfully. Think about what those changes were and whether or not they were successful.

- Describe the most satisfying aspects of doing your research and think about why you particularly enjoyed them. This might tell you things about possible avenues you might want to explore in the future.

- Now think about the main challenges you experienced, the barriers you needed to overcome and the strategies you used to overcome them. Coping well with setbacks and overcoming barriers helps us to develop resilience; an important personal quality for the future.

It is always good to look back and reflect on what you might have done differently. This is not about beating yourself up for things that you feel you should have done better, but rather learning from things to help you for next time. All research is a process that we can learn from, and even experienced researchers encounter things they don't expect and can't predict. As a first time researcher it is good to be aware of this and to know that such things are common.

Space for your thoughts

What have you learned about yourself?

Carrying out a research project means being able to work independently, and inevitably this means that you learn a lot about yourself in relation to a number of different areas that are linked with your personal qualities. Here are some of them, and you might be able to think of more:

- **Resilience** – the ability to bounce back and recover following a negative event or experience. Higgins (1994: 373) describes it as, 'The capacity to spring back, rebound, successfully adapt in the face of adversity, and develop social, academic and vocational competence despite exposure to severe stress or simply to the stress inherent in today's world'. Resilience is an important quality in all sorts of areas of life, and we develop it through experience.

- **Confidence** – linked with issues of self-belief. During your research project you may well have done things for the first time and tackled things that you have not experienced before. Hopefully these have been encouraging and have helped you to feel increasingly more secure in your abilities.

- **Work ethic** – working to the best of your ability. Completing your research project means that you have met your own targets and deadlines as well as those of the university. This shows you are conscientious and hard-working.

- **Initiative** – taking action without needing to be told or directed first. By this point you will have carried out a lot of work independently and you will have done much of this with minimal direction. This shows that you can think for yourself and act on the strength of your convictions.

- **Determination and persistence** – not giving up. A research project involves a big commitment, and reaching the final stages means you have both of these. If you didn't, you wouldn't be here!

Many of these qualities are valued by employers, so you may well find yourself including them in personal statements when applying for jobs.

Space for your thoughts

How have your skills developed?

Carrying out a research project provides a good opportunity to learn more about yourself, particularly in relation to skills. Now is a good time to think about the things you feel you can do that perhaps you were less sure about before.

Skills can be grouped into these categories:

* **Communication** – includes verbal (individuals and groups, formal and informal), written (your write-up, formal letters) and IT (email, text messaging). If you carried out qualitative research, you may have developed interview skills.

* **Numerical** – using mathematical information to express ideas or information. This includes using methods for statistical analysis of data collected through questionnaires or examining numerical data collected previously.

* **Relational** – working well with others. This includes how you worked with your supervisor, your research participants and your colleagues.

* **Project management** – the smooth running of your research project. This includes how you organised yourself and your work, as well as your skills of problem solving.

To learn more about yourself you could also carry out a SWOT or SWAIN analysis:

Strengths – things you do well

Weaknesses – things you find difficult or could learn to do better

Opportunities – things that are available to you that could help you to develop

Threats – things that could get in the way of your development.

In a SWAIN analysis, opportunities and threats are replaced by aspirations, interests and needs.

Aspirations – things you hope for in the future, including things you would like to achieve

Interests – things you enjoy doing

Needs – things you need to focus on to reach your potential.

Notes

....

....

....

....

....

....

....

....

....

....

....

....

....

.... ## Try this

.... It is also good to think about how other
people view us as well as how we view
.... ourselves. Now think about how one of
your colleagues and your supervisor would
.... describe you as a student or researcher.

....

Alex's journal 10

So, a while ago our research methods tutors said they want us to present our research in progress. But it doesn't count for anything – didn't go down too well! We did it today and quite a few people didn't bother turning up. Turns out it was their loss! I presented what I've done so far and explained it. Couldn't believe how it helped me to understand so much more about what I'm doing. The questions people asked were really good too – showed me where I need to do more work and where I was getting a bit preachy about single-use plastic. Was able to have a really good conversation with my supervisor too about some things I'm finding tricky at the moment. Definitely a bit nerve-wracking but definitely worth it!

Case Study

A fresh pair of eyes

Beth is in the final stages of writing up her qualitative research project and is checking through her work for errors. She has been in regular contact with her supervisor who has encouraged her to read Wolcott's work on writing up qualitative research (Wolcott, 2009). Beth found it useful and has referred to it in her methodology section.

Beth shows this section to her supervisor who points out that she has mis-spelt Wolcott's surname as Woolcott. Beth is not convinced by this but decides to say nothing and check the details in the library catalogue, secretly hoping to prove her supervisor wrong. Beth has looked at the book several times and is convinced she is right. When she checks the catalogue she discovers that the supervisor is right after all and she realises that it wouldn't have mattered how many times she looked at the book, she had read Woolcott and not Wolcott. She decides to ask a friend on a different course to proofread her work for errors as she now feels she can't see them any more.

Notes

....

....

....

....

....

Part 2 My research project

This part of the journal is designed to be more personal, and is structured around a series of key questions for you to reflect on in relation to your own research project. This section can be used alongside Part 1 or following it, depending on what suits you best. Either way, it will provide you with an important record that you can return to when you get to the writing-up stage.

1. The Research Process

Carrying out a research project is an iterative cycle, a cycle that you repeat more than once, possibly even several times, particularly in qualitative research. The Research Triangle describes a fundamental dimension of the research process that we need to engage with throughout the duration of any study and is depicted in Figure 10.

Figure 10: The Research Triangle

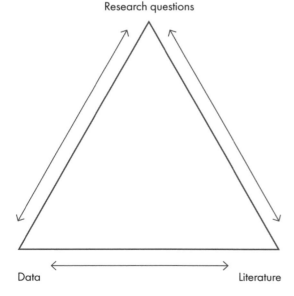

- Initial research questions are always written as part of a research proposal and give an indication of what to start reading, hence the arrow from Research questions to Literature down the right-hand side of the Triangle.

- A literature review means that questions might need to be amended in the light of what we have read, hence the arrow from Literature back to Research questions up the right-hand side of the Triangle.

- Research questions also act as a guide to the data we need to gather, hence the arrow from Research questions to Data down the left-hand side of the Triangle.

- As we gather the data, we do not always find what we expect, so again the Research questions are amended, hence the arrow from Data back to Research questions up the left-hand side of the Triangle.

- As we read, we find other possible areas of focus, so we might decide to amend some of the questions in our survey or interview schedule, and hence the arrow from Literature to Data along the base of the Triangle.

- The data gathered might point us to some specific areas we now need to include in our literature review, hence the arrow from Data back to Literature along the base of the Triangle.

This iterative process often means that you can't necessarily write a dissertation from start to finish, something that many people (including myself) find difficult. Often it involves reworking sections as your work develops. Frustrating as this might be at times, it may well lead to a better piece of work in the end. The process is also something that you can reflect on either in your methodology section or in a reflective evaluation of your research if you are asked to write one.

2. The introduction

In your introduction, it is likely that you will need to discuss the rationale for your project. Here are some reflective questions to help you to record your thoughts on this. To do this you need to go back to the beginning and think back to the early days of your study, or even before then if appropriate.

What made you want to carry out research in this particular area and where did your initial ideas come from? Here you will want to consider such things as your interest in the topic and what sparked it, what you had studied in this area before (for example, a previous module), what you had read on the topic and so on.

What makes you feel that this is an important area for you to focus on? This might relate to your personal values (see Theme 6.2), further study you would like to undertake and possible employment in the future. There may be some personal reasons too.

What are your research questions and how are they developing during the project? Have your research questions changed at all?

Now think about any assumptions you might have been making at the beginning of the project. What were they and how did you become aware of them? Did you feel you were looking for, or even wanting, particular answers to your research questions?

How did you challenge these assumptions?

Now think about the setting for your research. Where did you carry out your research and how did you choose it? How were your options limited?

If you undertook desk research or a literature review, think about what made you choose that particular option, and give your reasons here.

Now write a summary of the sections that will follow your introduction. Just headings will be fine at this point. This will give you a helpful, clear overview of your whole piece of work.

Top
Tip

A strong structure

It is generally not difficult to write about things that we find easy and to avoid writing about things we find difficult. This can ultimately lead to a piece of work that is unbalanced. In Theme 3.5 we discussed the number of words you might write in each section of your work; this kind of framework will ensure your work is well balanced. University assessment criteria cover all aspects of a dissertation. Scoring highly against all of them is likely to lead to a positive outcome.

Your dissertation guidelines will probably include some detail in relation to a structure to follow, and it is important not to deviate from that. However, within this structure, it is also good to think about how you will present each section of your work, and here are some pointers:

• Make sure each section has an introduction and a conclusion – the phrase, 'Say what you're going to say, say it and say what you've said' is useful, because it is a clear signpost to the reader. You may well want to add, 'Say what comes next' too.

• Headings and sub-headings – these also guide the reader through your work. Using the right number of these is important: not too many to break up your work and interfere with your arguments, and not too few, leaving lengthy amounts of text that might be difficult to follow.

• Don't be afraid to repeat your research questions – you won't need to do this in every section, but if they are only in your introduction, the reader will lose sight of them and have to go back to find them. A couple of timely reminders can work well.

• An abstract – if you are asked to write an abstract, be sure to summarise everything (even your findings).

Following the guidance given for the structure of your work should help you write a strong piece. However, if you do want to deviate from this for your particular piece of research, do discuss it with your supervisor first to be on the safe side.

3. Literature review

Writing an effective literature review is all about critically evaluating published material that relates to your research questions. Remember this can include textbooks, articles from academic journals, research reports, chapters from edited collections, information from reputable websites, magazines, newspapers and other sources as appropriate (such as films, video recordings and exhibitions).

Now think about what you have read and note down the top five key publications you have identified and rank them in order of importance. Make a note of the reasons for your choices. Now write a short summary of their contrasting arguments.

Why might these publications be particularly important in relation to your study?

Now think about the arguments in literature that you find the most convincing. What is convincing about them? What are the main counter-arguments to these?

Now think about the flaws that you have identified in the arguments being made (this could include things like a lack of evidence for the claims being made, more studies being needed in this particular area or a general lack of literature in this particular area).

Notes

Using annotated bibliographies

When reading a number of academic texts, compiling an annotated bibliography can be a helpful thing to do as part of a strategy for a literature review. An annotated bibliography is a list of things you have read, referenced in the appropriate style. Each reference is followed by a short description (usually about 150 words) of the text. Compiling an annotated bibliography will help you to:

- record key points in things you have read;

- identify literature you do not need to refer to because you can't describe its relevance to your study;

- continue practising referencing in the appropriate style.

You may be asked to write an annotated bibliography as part of the research process. Even if you aren't, it can be a useful thing to do anyway. You can take it along to a supervision session to refer to in your discussions.

Notes

....

....

....

....

....

....

....

....

....

....

....

....

....

....

4. Methodology

Imagine you are in a coffee shop talking to a student in the year below about your research project. They are starting to think about theirs and have asked you to describe what you did and why. They would like you to tell them about the ups and downs, what worked well and what didn't, and what you would do differently if you were in their shoes. Write freely about what you would say.

In Theme 5 you were introduced to a hierarchy of research objectives. Figure 11 is a copy of Figure 7 but the boxes have been left blank. Insert the words from this list into the correct upper boxes:

Positivist
Qualitative
Epistemology (twice)
Objectivist
Quantitative
Research methods (twice)
Subjectivist
Ontology (twice)
Interpretivist

Then complete the lower boxes from this list:

A number of solutions
Answer
Appliance of science
Cannot be proved
Descriptions
Explain
Explains objective descriptions
Explore
Explores subjective reasons
Factual
Focus group
Insights
Interpretation of data
Interview
Multiple answers
Multiple realities
No universal laws
Numerical data
Observation
One correct answer
One single reality
One solution
Opinion
Provable
Questionnaire
Reasons
Recommendations
Solution
Survey
Universal laws
Verbal data
What happens
Why things happen

Figure 11: Your hierachy of research objectives

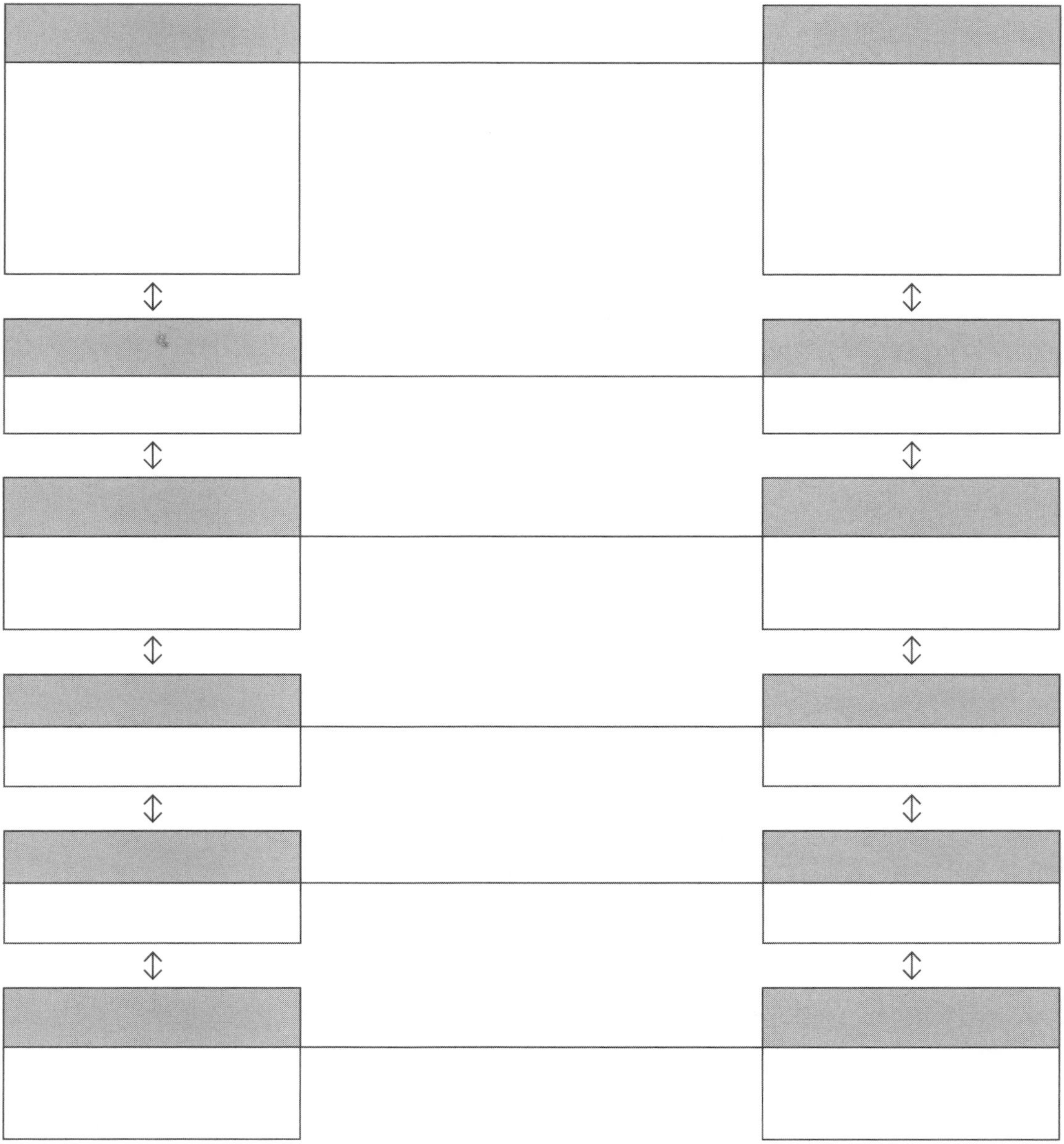

Using Figure 11, now think about each of these questions.

What is your methodological paradigm?

How and why is this relevant for your research?

What is your research method and why is this relevant for your research?

Which research methods are you using?

Now think about the ethical issues you are facing in your research, such as confidentiality, gaining informed consent, keeping data safe and causing no harm to participants. You may have others too.

How are you addressing these?

How would you describe your position within the research?

What assumptions might you be making now?

How will you challenge your assumptions?

'Put yourself in my shoes'

When planning your research, it is good to imagine that you are a participant and to think about how you would ideally like to be treated. This will help you to highlight any ethical issues that might affect how you carry out the research. It might raise these points, and you might be able to think of more:

- **Being taken seriously** – I am sharing things about myself (for example, my views, opinions, experiences), so I want my data to be valued and regarded as useful whatever I might share.

- **Non-judgemental** – I do not want anyone to judge me for what I share.

- **Honesty** – I want my data to be represented accurately and not to be twisted or adapted in any way that would misrepresent me, even if it is not what I am expected to share.

- **Anonymous** – I do not want anyone to be able to recognise me in the study.

- **Private** – I do not want anyone else to hear about my data, for example in the coffee shop.

- **Confidential** – I want my data stored safely and securely where nobody can access it.

- **Support** – if I find taking part in the research difficult in some way, I want to know who I can talk to.

- **Withdrawal** – if things get difficult or I no longer wish to take part, I would like to be able to withdraw.

All universities have ethical codes for carrying out research, designed to safeguard you and your participants.

5. Data analysis

Once you have gathered your data (or sometimes even during data gathering) you will need to start the process of analysing it. Here are some reflective questions to help you to think about how to make progress in this area:

Which methods and techniques for analysis are you considering?

Which have you selected and why?

What are the main things that your data is telling you?

Select a minimum of three key themes from your data and explain why you selected them.

What insights does your data give you in relation to your research questions?

What does your data tell you that is new or different?

Are there any gaps that you can identify?

Case Study

Selecting the most significant data

George is really pleased with how his research is going. He has gathered lots of useful qualitative data through some semi-structured interviews and he now faces the task of analysing the transcriptions to see what insights this gives him into his research question. George is pleased because the data seems to speak for itself. He organises it into ten themes and discusses each briefly, being sure to include lots of direct quotations from the transcripts to reflect clearly what the participants said.

George takes his analysis along to his next supervision session and feels that his work on it is complete. However, his supervisor feels that because he has so many themes, he has only skimmed the surface of his data, making the whole section descriptive rather than analytical. The supervisor explains that he needs to be much more selective, choosing the themes that are the most significant and analysing these in depth. George is upset because this means he will not be able to include all his data, something that his supervisor says is almost inevitable in qualitative research.

Notes

....

....

....

....

6. Discussion

Having carried out your data analysis, you may need to write a discussion section, making links back with the literature in your review. Here are some questions to help you to do this.

Go back to the five key texts that you identified in Table 3 on page 57. Now think about how far your research confirms what is discussed there.

Where are the contradictions (things you didn't find)?

Are there any gaps?

Were you surprised by anything you discovered?

Case Study

From data description to data analysis

Nadia has analysed her quantitative data and is in the process of writing her discussion section. She is making links back to her hypothesis and the literature in her review; she soon feels that her work is becoming repetitive and she wonders what to do about this. She emails her supervisor for advice and they highlight that it is important that she writes it as an analytical commentary rather than simply repeating herself. The supervisor points out that a good discussion section is often relatively short and succinct; it is important to state the findings, show the relevant results and link this back to appropriate literature. Nadia is also advised to focus on any conflicting data and any unexpected findings to make her work stronger.

Notes

....

....

....

....

....

....

7. Conclusions

Writing your conclusions probably means you are reaching the end of the research process. Here are some questions to help you to do this well.

> Imagine you are talking to the student in the year below again and they ask you to summarise your findings. What would you say about these? Try and keep it to no more than 100 words.
>
> Now highlight your recommendations and again describe them briefly here.
>
> Which of your findings do you feel is the most significant and why?
>
> What further research could you do to move thinking in this area forward?

Notes

Case Study

Time to celebrate together

Jerome, Chloe and Luca became friends in their first year and are now in their final year. They are all on different courses and spend a lot of time working independently on their dissertations. They all like to work in the library and it is always good to see one another there. This really helps their motivation and they often meet up to discuss their progress as well as to have coffee and go out and relax together. As their time at university comes to an end they feel it will soon be time to celebrate. They start talking about what they will do on their graduation day. Chloe suggests that they could all go out together after the ceremony with their families, and they all feel this is a good idea. On the day, they enjoy celebrating together and are thankful for the support they have had and for the great friendships they have made.

Notes

References

Adams, J.S. (1965) 'Inequality is social exchange' in L. Berkowitz (ed) *Advances in Experimental Psychology*, New York: Academic Press, pp 267–99.

Allen, D. (2015) *Getting Things Done: The Art of Stress-Free Productivity*, London: Piatkus.

Argyris, C. (1982) *Reasoning, Learning and Action: Individual and Organizational*, San Francisco: Jossey-Bass.

Aveyard, H. (2018) *Doing a Literature Review in Health and Social Care: A Practical Guide*, London: Open University Press.

Balnaves, M. and Caputi, P. (2001) *Introduction to Quantitative Research Methods: An Investigative Approach*, London: Sage.

Bassot, B. (2016) *The Reflective Practice Guide*, Abingdon: Routledge.

Bassot, B. (2019) *The Study Success Journal*, London: Red Globe Press.

Beauchamp, T.L. and Childress, J.F. (2013) *Principles of Biomedical Ethics* (7th edn), Oxford: Oxford University Press.

Bell, J. and Waters, S. (2018) *Doing Your Research Project: A Guide for First-Time Researchers* (7th edn), London: Open University Press.

Bergin, T. (2018) *An Introduction to Data Analysis: Quantitative, Qualitative and Mixed Methods*, London: Sage.

Biggam, J. (2018) *Succeeding with Your Master's Dissertation: A Step-by-Step Guide* (4th edn), London: Open University Press.

Bliss, E.C. (2018) *Doing it Now: A 12-Step Program for Curing Procrastination and Achieving your Goals*, New York: Charles Scribner's Sons.

Bolton, G. and Delderfield, R. (2018) *Reflective Practice: Writing and Professional Development*, London: Sage.

Booth, A., Sutton, A. and Papaionnou, D. (2016) *Systematic Approaches to a Successful Literature Review* (2nd edn), London: Sage.

Borg, S. (2001) 'The research journal: a tool for promoting and understanding researcher development', *Language Teaching Research*, 5(2): 156–77.

Boud, D., Keogh, R. and Walker, D. (1985) *Reflection: Turning Experience into Learning*, London: RoutledgeFalmer.

Bryman, A. (2016) *Social Research Methods* (5th edn), Oxford: Oxford University Press.

Cohen, L., Manion, L. and Morrison, K. (2017) *Research Methods in Education* (8th edn), Abingdon: Routledge.

Cottrell, S. (2014) *Dissertations and Project Reports: A Step-by-Step Guide*, Basingstoke: Palgrave Macmillan.

Coughlan, M. and Cronin, P. (2016) *Doing a Literature Review in Nursing*, Health and Social Care (2nd edn), London: Sage.

Covey, S. (2004) T*he 7 Habits of Highly Effective People*, London: Pocket Books.

Creswell, J.W. and Creswell, J.D. (2018) *Research Design: Qualitative, Quantitative and Mixed Methods Approaches* (5th edn), Thousand Oaks, CA: Sage.

Denscombe, M. (2017) *The Good Research Guide for Small-Scale Social Research Projects* (5th edn), Maidenhead: Open University Press.

Denzin, N.K. and Lincoln, Y.S. (2017) *The Sage Handbook of Qualitative Research* (5th edn), Thousand Oaks, CA: Sage.

Drucker, P. (1954) *The Practice of Management*, New York: Harper & Row.

Eales-Reynolds, L.-J., Judge, B., McCreery, E. and Jones, P. (2013) *Critical Thinking Skills for Education Students* (2nd edn), London: Sage.

Finley, S. (2008) 'Characteristics of community-based research', in L.M. Given (ed), *Sage Encyclopedia of Qualitative Research Methods* (Volumes 1 and 2), Thousand Oaks, CA: Sage.

Fook, J. and Askeland, G.A. (2006) 'The "critical" in critical reflection', in S. White, J. Fook and F. Gardner (eds), *Critical Reflection in Health and Social Care*, Maidenhead: Open University Press/ McGraw-Hill Education, pp 40–54.

Greetham, B. (2019) *How to Write your Undergraduate Dissertation* (3rd edn), London: Red Globe Press.

Heale, R. and Twycross, A. (2015) 'Validity and reliability in quantitative studies', *Evidence-Based Nursing*, 18(3): 66–7.

Higgins, G. (1994) *Resilient Adults: Overcoming a Cruel Past*, San Francisco: Jossey-Bass.

Kara, H. (2018) *Research Ethics in the Real World*, Bristol: Policy Press.

Koh, A.W.L., Lee, S.C. and Lim, S.W.H. (2018) 'The learning benefits of teaching: a retrieval practice hypothesis', *Applied Cognitive Psychology*, 32(3): 401–10.

Korstjens, I. and Moser, A. (2018) '"Trustworthiness and publishing" in Part 4: Practical guidance to qualitative research', *European Journal of General Practice*, 24(1): 120–4.

Luft, H. (1984) *Group Processes: An Introduction to Group Dynamics*, Mountain View, CA: Mayfield.

Mantell, A. and Scragg, T. (2019) *Reflective Practice in Social Work* (5th edn), London: Learning Matters (Sage).

Maslow, A.H. (1954) *Motivation and Personality*, New York: Harper and Row.

McGregor, G. (1970) *The Human Side of Enterprise*, Maidenhead: McGraw-Hill.

Mueller, P.A. and Oppenheimer, D.M. (2014) 'The pen is mightier than the keyboard: advantages of longhand over laptop note taking', *Psychological Science*, 25(6): 1159–68.

Noble, H. and Smith, J. (2015) 'Issues of validity and reliability in qualitative research', *Evidence-Based Nursing*, 18(2): 34–5.

Oliver, P. (2010) *The Student's Guide to Research Ethics* (2nd edn), Maidenhead: Open University Press.

Oliver, P. (2012) *Succeeding with Your Literature Review: A Handbook for Students*, Maidenhead: Open University Press.

Ortlipp, M. (2008) 'Keeping and using reflective journals in the qualitative research process', *The Qualitative Report*, 13(4): 696–705.

Pears, R. and Shields, G. (2019) *Cite Them Right: The Essential Referencing Guide*, London: Red Globe Press.

Pérez Alonso, M.A. (2015) 'Metacognition and sensorimotor components underlying the process of handwriting and keyboarding and their impact on learning: an analysis from the perspective of embodied psychology', *Procedia – Social and Behavioral Sciences*, 176: 263–9.

Peters, S. (2012) *The Chimp Paradox*, London: Vermilion.

Pink, D. (2009) *Drive: The Surprising Truth about What Motivates Us*, New York: Riverhead Books.

Punch, K.F. (2014) *Introduction to Social Research: Quantitative and Qualitative Approaches* (3rd edn), London: Sage.

Riches, A. (2012) 'Where Did That Come From?' *How to Keep Control in Any Situation*, e-book, Sudbury, MA: eBookIt. Available at: www.anneriches.com.au/almond-effect.html

Ridley, D. (2012) *The Literature Review: A Step-by-Step Guide for Students* (2nd edn), London: Sage.

Thomas, G. (2017) *How to Do Your Research Project: A Guide for Students in Education and Applied Social Sciences* (3rd edn), London: Sage.

Thompson, N. (2012) *The People Solutions Sourcebook*, Basingstoke: Palgrave Macmillan.

Tracy, B. (2017) *Eat that Frog! 21 Great Ways to Stop Procrastination and Get More Done in Less Time* (3rd edn), Oakland, CA: Berrett-Koehler.

van Emden, J. and Becker, L. (2016) *Presentation Skills for Students* (3rd edn), Palgrave Macmillan: Basingstoke.

Vroom, V.H. (1964) *Work and Motivation*, New York: John Wiley.

Wayback Machine (2014) *Internet archive*. Available at: https://archive.org/web/

White, P. (2017) *Developing Research Questions* (2nd edn), Palgrave Macmillan: Basingstoke.

Wolcott, H.F. (2009) *Writing up Qualitative Research* (3rd edn), Thousand Oaks, CA: Sage.

Index

word count 48–49
   writing 51
transferability 74
trustworthiness 74
Twycross, A. 74
typing 16–17

U

university library catalogue 56

V

validity 74
van Emden, J. 146
vision for research 26–27
visual aids 146
Vroom, V.H. 130

W

Walker, D. 136
Wayback Machine 118
White, P. 35
Wolcott, H.F. 155
word count 48–49
work ethic 150
writing 16–17, 51
   free-flow writing 12
   reflective 18–23
   word count 48–59
   see also journal writing
written consent 92

X

X and Y theory 130